pretty little
patchwork

LARK

SENIOR EDITOR
Valerie Van Arsdale Shrader

EDITOR
Larry Shea

ART DIRECTOR
Megan Kirby

COVER DESIGNER
Carol Morse Barnao

ILLUSTRATOR
Susan McBride

PHOTOGRAPHER
Stewart O'Shields

An Imprint of Sterling Publishing
387 Park Avenue South
New York, NY 10016

First Paperback Edition 2013
Text © 2008, Lark Books
Photography © 2008, Lark Books unless otherwise specified
Illustrations ©2008, Lark Books unless otherwise specified

The Library of Congress has cataloged the hardcover edition as follows:
Pretty little patchwork / [Valerie Shrader, editor].
    p. cm.
Includes index.
ISBN 13: 978-1-60059-213-3 (hardcover) 978-1-4547-0856-8 (paperback)
1. Patchwork. 2. Quilting. I. Shrader, Valerie Van Arsdale.
TT835.P72 2008
746.46'041--dc22

2007047231

Distributed in Canada by Sterling Publishing
c/o Canadian Manda Group, 165 Dufferin Street
Toronto, Ontario, Canada M6K 3H6
Distributed in the United Kingdom by GMC Distribution Services
Castle Place, 166 High Street, Lewes, East Sussex, England BN7 1XU
Distributed in Australia by Capricorn Link (Australia) Pty. Ltd.
P.O. Box 704, Windsor, NSW 2756, Australia

For information about custom editions, special sales, and premium and corporate purchases, please contact Sterling Special Sales at 800-805-5489 or specialsales@sterlingpublishing.com.

Email academic@larkbooks.com for information about desk and examination copies. The complete policy can be found at larkcrafts.com.

Every effort has been made to ensure that all the information in this book is accurate. However, due to differing conditions, tools, and individual skills, the publisher cannot be responsible for any injuries, losses, and other damages that may result from the use of the information in this book.

Manufactured in Canada

2 4 6 8 10 9 7 5 3 1

larkcrafts.com

contents

introduction

*P*atchwork isn't just about quilts anymore. It's about using what you have—think fabric scraps—and loving what you make. And it doesn't have to be quaint or traditional. No, the new patchwork is all about playfulness, functionality, and, as you'll soon discover in the pages of this book, *personality*.

Not to mention possibility. Thanks to the pool of talented designers who created the projects in this book, you'll find 32 reasons to stitch together something pretty—for yourself, your home, and even your laptop. And because the designs in this book are timeless, they look great in any setting. Plus, you can customize any project with your own fabric combinations and finally use up all those pretty little scraps you've been saving. (Of course, you can also indulge in fabulous new fabrics, too.)

We kick things off with the basics section, which tells you what tools and materials to gather and teaches you the easy techniques you'll need to get started. Patchwork is simply the piecing together of fabrics, after all. Then it's on to the fun part: the fabulous projects you can make. All of them appear in full-color photos with easy-to-follow instructions that take the "work" out of patchwork. Need an eye-catching addition to your outfit? You'll find funky belts, a headband that will turn heads, a sassy clutch, and more. How about something for your home? Spruce it up with sweet picture frames, down-home coasters, and—as a nod to patchwork's humble past—a

mod little art quilt that's perfectly suited for beginners. If it's a special I-can't-believe-you-made-this-yourself gift that you're looking for, check out some scented sachets, starry pincushions, sure-to-be-treasured ornaments, and—well, pretty much every project in the book.

One look at these exciting projects and you'll be bursting at the seams to get started. So dig through your stash of fabrics and get inspired. All you need is this book and a little free time.

Piece, love, and patchwork.

patchwork basics

This chapter will put you in the know about the tools, materials, and techniques you'll need to make the projects in this book. Even if you're an experienced sewer, you'll find tidbits here that will enable you to create your patchwork items faster and easier. If you're a beginner, you'll want to read this section carefully and refer to it often. Whether expert or novice, you should start by gathering the items in the Basic Patchwork Tool Kit. Many of the tools and materials in it can probably already be found among your sewing supplies.

Beyond the basic kit, you'll learn here about the other tools and the wonderful range of materials you'll use, depending on which projects strike your fancy. Just as you probably have most of the essential tools on hand, you'll find that a quick rummage through your sewing materials (and perhaps your junk drawer) will uncover all sorts of scraps, odds, and ends you can transform into prized pieces of patchwork.

patchworktools

In this section, we'll run through the essential items that make up the tool kit.

ROTARY CUTTER AND MAT

If you're a longtime patchworker or quilter, the rotary cutter has something in common with things like cell phones, e-mail, and late afternoon double lattes. You know you must have functioned somehow before they came along, but you're not sure exactly how.

Together with a transparent ruler or straightedge and a self-healing cutting mat, the rotary cutter makes short work of cutting fabric pieces—lots of them—to just the right size. If you've never used a rotary cutter, try one at your local fabric store. In general, the larger the rotary blade, the easier it is to cut fabric. A mid-size cutter will do the job for the projects in this book.

MAKING THE CUT

When cutting, use a mat and ruler and hold the rotary cutter at a 45° angle, with the blade set firmly against the ruler's edge. Keep even pressure on the cutter, and always cut away from yourself. When not in use, use the safety latch and follow the manufacturer's instructions when it's time to replace the blades.

BASIC PATCHWORK TOOL KIT

- Rotary cutter and mat
- Measuring tape
- Transparent ruler
- Sharp sewing scissors (for fabric)
- Sharp fine-tipped scissors (for detailed work)
- Craft scissors (for paper)
- Fabric-marking pen or pencil and tailor's chalk
- Straight pins
- Hand-sewing needles
- Scrap paper (for patterns)
- Sewing machine
- Sewing machine needles
- Seam ripper
- Iron

MEASURING TAPE AND TRANSPARENT RULER

For measuring out larger pieces of fabric to cut, a measuring tape is all you need. A transparent quilting ruler holds down several jobs without breaking a sweat: You can use one to measure and mark precise distances, determine a perpendicular line to your fabric's edge, and guide a rotary cutter straight and sure.

SHARP SEWING SCISSORS

Even if you have a rotary cutter to cut pieces to size, good-quality sewing scissors are still an essential part of your sewing kit. You'll need two pairs. For basic cuts, a pair of 7- or 8-inch (17.8 or 20.3 cm) dressmaker's bent-handled shears will do the job. The design of the handle allows the fabric to lay flat as you cut. To cut tight curves and do other detail work like trimming seams, a pair of fine-tipped, 4- or 5-inch (10.2 or 12.7 cm) sewing scissors is the way to go.

THIS TIME, PAPER BEATS SCISSORS

Never let anyone—including yourself in a hurried moment—use your good sewing scissors to cut paper. The wood fibers in the paper will dull the blades quickly and make them useless on fabric.

CRAFT SCISSORS

Just as sewing scissors are meant for fabric and thread, craft scissors are perfect for paper. You'll need a pair of them to cut out the templates in several patchwork projects. Find a pair that feels comfortable in your hand. A short to moderate length is best for making fine cuts on curves and corners.

FABRIC-MARKING PEN OR PENCIL AND TAILOR'S CHALK

You'll want to use a water-soluble fabric marker for marking lines for cutting, embroidering, and sewing. The ink should vanish with plain water, but test your pen on a scrap piece of fabric first, as the dyes in some fabrics can make the ink hard to remove. Besides fabric-marking pens, a variety of fabric chalks— both traditional and newfangled—are available.

STRAIGHT PINS

Any basic dressmaker's pins will work for holding fabric pieces in place when sewing. Longer ones with plastic or glass heads are easier to handle, and easier on your fingertips. They're also easier to spot and remove as you stitch your way past them.

HAND-SEWING NEEDLES

A variety pack of needles should include all the types you need for the projects in this book. You'll want to use a finer needle for lightweight fabrics and a thicker, longer needle for thicker fabrics. Regular woven fabrics and silks do best with the sharp pointed needles known—unsurprisingly—as "sharps." Round-tipped needles, or "ball-points," are better for knit materials, as the rounded point pushes between the fibers without piecing them, which can cause a run or pull.

Some projects in the book ask specifically for an embroidery needle. This type has a longer eye to make it easier to thread several strands of embroidery floss at once. You can use embroidery needles for detailing and for regular hand stitching as well.

SEAM RIPPER

Everybody makes mistakes at least once in a while, so this handy tool is essential. It easily removes incorrect stitches without anyone being the wiser.

DON'T DO THE TWIST

Tired of licking and twisting thread ends trying to get them—steady now!—through a needle's eye? Instead, just use that handy helper known as a needle threader. Pull its wire loop through the needle, insert the thread, pull back, and you're ready to sew.

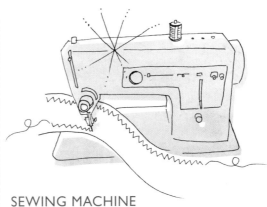

SEWING MACHINE

To make the many seams patchwork requires, a sewing machine is impossible to beat for speed and efficiency. If you're sewing thicker fabrics, be sure to use longer stitches and to reduce the pressure on the presser foot to allow the fabric to glide through the machine. For raw edges, a zigzag stitch keeps the fabric from fraying.

SEWING MACHINE NEEDLES

Always keep extra sewing machine needles on hand. Just as sharp scissors make cutting fabrics a piece of cake, it's easier to sew with sharp needles. It's a good idea to use a new needle at the beginning of each sewing project. That way you won't be using a dull needle in the middle of it.

IRON

Beyond its everyday job of getting out wrinkles, an iron can take on a number of tasks in the patchwork process. You can use it to apply interfacings and appliqués, and to press seams open.

optional tools

Some of the following tools will make an occasional cameo appearance in the projects in this book, while others will be frequent supporting stars for the everyday tools above.

PINKING SHEARS

Pinking shears have a serrated edge and leave a zigzag pattern that can help limit fraying. You can also use them to make decorative cuts and edges.

GLUE AND ADHESIVES

Besides just thread, the projects you'll find ahead use a variety of methods to connect pieces of fabric together. These include such items as spray adhesive, white glue, glue sticks, and hot glue with a glue gun. The right one to use depends on the amount of strength, durability, and quickness of setting the project requires.

ASSORTED OTHER TOOLS

As you browse through the "What You Need" lists in the projects, a variety of other tools will pop up. These include:

* A craft knife, sometimes used to cut out templates

* An embroidery hoop, to hold fabric taut as you detail it

* A knitting needle or chopstick, to push out corners

* A funnel, to neatly add stuffing material

* A staple gun, to attach material to a frame

Many of these tools are probably already somewhere around your house. A few tools employed in the projects are a little more specialized—for example, a loop turner, which is a slender metal rod you use to turn bias tubing inside out.

PRETTY IN PINKING

Hold your pinking shears straight when cutting fabric and close the blades completely to make a full cut. If a fabric is too delicate for pinking, place it on top of a sturdier fabric and pink through both layers.

patchwork materials

Because patchwork can employ pieces of fabric in just about any size, shape, or pattern, you almost certainly already have some materials on hand. It's just a question of seeing what fabrics you need to add to your selection, and which specialized materials—like batting or interfacing—require a trip to the fabric store.

FABRIC VARIETIES

Natural fabrics are usually your best bet. Cotton in particular is always a safe choice and is used in many of the projects in this book. Here's a brief description of the fabrics you'll encounter in the projects:

CHARMING QUARTERS

Two terms to know before heading to the fabric store: Charm squares are squares of fabric cut to predetermined sizes, with 5 inches (12.7 cm) square a common size. A fat quarter is a half-yard of fabric that has been cut in half so that each piece measures approximately 18 x 21 inches (45.7 x 53.3 cm).

COTTON

Cotton is durable, easy to sew, and has a soft, natural feel. Luckily for your patchwork combinations, it comes in an endless array of colors and prints. Cotton is more likely to shrink than many other fabrics, so pre-washing it is a must.

CANVAS

Canvas is a heavy-duty fabric used for sails, tents, and backpacks. It's a great choice for making sturdier patchwork projects. In the United States, canvas is graded by weight (ounces per square yard) and by number. The numbers run in reverse of the weight, so number 10 canvas is lighter than number 4.

LINEN

Linen is lustrous, strong, and durable. Like cotton, you can find it in an assortment of wonderful colors and prints. Also like cotton, linen is prone to wrinkling, so it's best to press your fabric both before and after sewing to have a smooth surface.

SILK

Sturdy is all well and good, but how about adding a little luxury to your projects? Silk offers a refined touch and a lustrous look. Choose a medium-weight silk that can stand up to some wear and tear, and be sure to use a sharp, new needle when sewing. Silk also ravels or frays easily, so seams should be finished.

FELT

As materials go, felt is pretty much foolproof. It's non-woven, soft, doesn't ravel, and has no right side or wrong side to worry about. Traditionally, felt is made from wool, though the felt you see in craft stores is usually synthetic.

WOOL

Speaking of wool: this classic fabric can be fuzzy or smooth, and fleecy or ribbed. It's soft, durable, and very absorbent.

SELECTING COLORS AND PATTERNS

In choosing your types of fabrics, you consider qualities like workability and durability (yawn!). When it comes to picking colors, however, the most essential quality is fun. Another thing to keep in mind with colors, though, is how well they work together in your patchwork composition.

Values, also known as tones, refer to the lightness or darkness of a color, not its particular hue. When combining colors, you can choose between medium or darker tones or lighter, more pastel values. Whether you seek to match all the values in a piece or create dramatic juxtapositions is up to you.

Besides the colors themselves, you need to choose from among solids, stripes and patterns. Just be sure you're aware of what effect the mixture of colors and patterns you choose produces. No one piece should visually stand out from all the others—unless you decide you want it to!

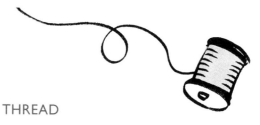

THREAD

Bargain thread is no bargain. Your best bet is to buy a quality polyester thread for your machine and hand sewing to create strong seams that will remain that way. A good-quality all-cotton thread can also work well with the woven, natural fabrics (like cotton, for example) used in most of the projects in this book.

EMBROIDERY FLOSS

Embroidery floss is a decorative thread that comes in six loosely twisted strands. You can buy it in cotton, silk, rayon, or other fibers and in every color of the rainbow. You'll use an embroidery needle to sew decorative stitches with it.

STAND BACK, LOOK CLOSE

When combining different fabrics and colors, make sure of your choices before you sew them all together—you really don't want to be using that seam ripper. Place your different fabrics in position, and take a few steps back to see how the colors and contrasting patterns look together. One trick sometimes used by painters is to squint at your composition to see if anything leaps out visually.

LAYERING AND STUFFING MATERIALS

Unlike in quilts, where a middle layer is to be expected, not all patchwork projects require a filling between the outside layers of fabric. When they do, a common choice is cotton batting. It's durable, easy to work with, and available in different thicknesses. Felt is another option, depending on the thickness and feel you're looking for.

Some patchwork projects, like pillows, require stuffing. Polyester fiberfill is a good choice that keeps its shape well. Grade one variety is soft, resilient, and non-allergenic; it's easily available at craft and sewing stores.

INTERFACING

You can add support and structure to your projects with interfacing. The type used most often in the projects here is fusible interfacing, which means that you apply it by using the heat and pressure of an iron. Paper-back fusible web is a material that bonds on both sides when set with heat. It's useful for making appliqués.

PIPING

Piping is that round edging often used in furniture upholstery. It makes a great accent for pillows, pincushions, potholders, and even some things that don't begin with the letter P. To make your own piping, buy the inner cord at a fabric store, wrap it in a bias strip that matches or contrasts your piece, and stitch close to the cording. You can also buy ready-made piping.

RICKRACK AND RIBBONS

Rickrack is a great material for easily adding curvy detail and creative edging to your patchwork. And, as every crafter (and gift wrapper) knows, you can never have too much ribbon. Think outside the spool and try different varieties of ribbon such as velvet and grosgrain.

BEADS AND BUTTONS

Talk about unlimited options for decorating your patchwork! Just walk into any bead or fabric store and see how many choices you have. Buttons can be sewn on as is, or you can purchase specially made blanks for buttons and cover them with a fabric of your choice.

patchwork techniques

Tools and materials at the ready, it's almost time for the (sewing) pedal to hit the metal. First, though, here are some techniques and tips you'll need to know to make the patchwork creations that follow.

CUTTING OUT PATCHWORK PIECES

Before cutting up your patchwork components, prepare your fabrics. Wash your fabrics before starting on a project. This is especially important for fabrics that may shrink significantly, like cotton, or that have colors that might bleed (ruining that careful color combination you've just created). Press the fabric while it is still damp to remove any creases.

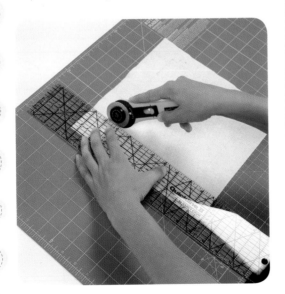

You can then measure your pieces with a measuring tape or ruler, and cut them with sewing scissors. Or—and this really pays off when you have many pieces to cut—you can cut them with a rotary cutter, self-healing cutting mat, and see-through fabric ruler as follows:

1 If the fabric has an uneven edge, straighten it by placing the ruler about 1/2 inch over the edge, making sure the ruler is at right angles to the straight grain of the fabric.

2 Place the rotary cutter against the ruler at the place on the fabric nearest you. Holding the cutter at a 45-degree angle—and pressing down on the ruler with your other hand—wheel the cutter away from you along the ruler's edge.

3 Once you have a straightened edge, you can cut the pieces you need individually. To do it most efficiently, cut strips to the width you need, place several on top of one another, and cut them together. Depending on the fabric weight, about four to six pieces can be cut at once. If you have to force the cutter to cut through the layers, try using fewer pieces at a time.

SAFETY FIRST AND SECOND

Why do rotary cutters work so beautifully? They're sharp! Two safety tips: First, keep the safety latch in place when the cutter is not in use. Second, always cut away from yourself, making sure to keep the fingers holding down the fabric or ruler out of harm's way.

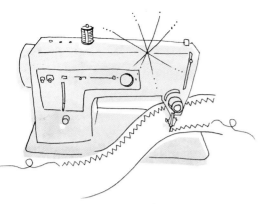

MACHINE STITCHING

Before we begin to make patchwork, let's discuss some sewing basics. When using a sewing machine, make sure the sewing tension is set properly for the fabric you are using. Test a scrap of fabric (never in short supply when patchworking) before getting to work on the real thing. Then follow these basic steps:

1 Pin the fabric pieces to each other with straight pins placed at right angles to the seam. Right sides should be together and edges properly aligned.

2 Machine stitch to the correct seam allowance, removing pins as you go.

3 To stitch around a corner, keep the needle down at the corner point and pivot the fabric.

4 When machine stitching, be sure to let the machine do the work of pulling the fabric along.

DON'T FORGET YOUR ALLOWANCE

Most of the projects in this book call for a seam allowance of 1/4 inch (0.6 cm). Pay close attention when a different allowance is required.

CLIPPING CORNERS AND CURVES

When you sew a piece inside out, the material in the seam allowance can bunch together when turned right side out. Luckily, getting rid of all that bulk and preventing the dreaded bunchiness is just a few snips away.

For fabric on a corner, before you turn the material right side out, clip straight across the seam allowance, halfway between the stitching and the corner of the fabric (figure 1).

For fabric on a curve, snip about two-thirds of the way into the seam allowance in several places (figure 2). This will allow the fabric to overlap slightly where it was snipped. The result is a smoother curve and seam on the right side.

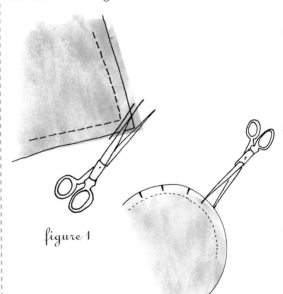

figure 1

figure 2

BASIC PIECING

Patchwork consists of pieces of fabric that are stitched together. They can be very symmetrical and stitched together to make even squares or rows, or they can be stitched in a more free-form manner.

When sewing rows of fabric squares together, pin the first two squares together, right sides facing, then stitch along the edge using the desired seam allowance. Add more squares in the same way. When your row is complete, pin and sew the rows together. Press seam allowances as you go to ensure more accurate piecing.

STRIP PIECING

One common (and easy) method for piecing fabric together is called strip piecing. You can use this technique to combine a number of rectangular strips into one larger piece. Just follow these steps:

1 Place your strips right sides up in the position they will be in the final piece. Put a needle through the left piece with the point sticking straight up (figure 1). This will be your "guide pin."

figure 1

2 Stitch the left piece (the one with the guide pin) to the one next to it, right sides together and the two near edges aligned. Turn the stitched piece to the right side (figure 2).

figure 2

3 Continue stitching pieces together (second to third, and so on) until the larger piece is complete. To check that you are stitching the correct edges together, just put your piece back down with the guide pin on the left and pointing up before you pick up the next strip to be attached. Finish by pressing open all the seams at once.

SENSE OF DIRECTION

The idea of a guide pin, described here for strip piecing, is one you can use elsewhere in patchwork. If you have trouble keeping track of the order or orientation of your pieces, pinning one to show its proper direction and position can help keep you on course.

FOUNDATION PIECING

Another way of assembling smaller pieces into a larger whole is called foundation piecing. This technique involves sewing fabric pieces onto a foundation of fabric (often muslin or lightweight cotton) or paper. A simple example of this method follows:

1 Place your foundation flat on your working surface. Lay down the first piece you're sewing onto it, with right side up and with its outer left edge flush with the edge of the foundation (figure 1). Working consistently left to right helps to avoid confusion. Stitch the first piece to the foundation along its outer edge.

figure 1

2 Position the second piece on top of the first, with right sides together and right edges aligned (figure 2). Stitch through all layers (the two pieces and the foundation) along this right-hand edge with a ¼-inch seam allowance. Press the seam flat, and then press the second piece to the right.

figure 2

3 Add your third piece just as you did the second piece in step 2. Repeat until all pieces are stitched to the foundation. To finish the piece, trim the top and bottom edges and machine-baste along the perimeter.

QUILTING

Quilting is the process of sandwiching batting between two layers of fabric and stitching through all the layers to create a decorative, textured effect. Some projects in this book are quilted, and this can be easily done on any sewing machine.

Whenever you are quilting, you need to make sure the layers are all held in the proper position. You can add basting stitches (long running stitches). Begin in the middle and smooth out all the layers as much as you can. Another way to hold the layers together as you work is to use temporary spray fabric adhesive.

The quilting stitches themselves can be made by hand or by a machine. You usually quilt in straight lines or curved patterns. For those who always refused to color inside the lines with their crayons, a more advanced technique known as free-motion quilting allows you to use stitches to create more random or elaborate designs.

HAND STITCHES

We've talked a lot about machine stitching, as that's very likely to be your main method for sewing patchwork. But even the most dedicated sewing-machine-head will need to make some stitches by hand. Here are those you may need to know for the projects in this book.

APPLIQUÉ STITCH

To camouflage the stitching holding on an appliqué, poke the needle through the base fabric and up through the appliqué, right next to the fold of the turned-under edge of the fabric. Bring the needle back down into the base fabric just a wee bit away. Repeat, as shown in figure 1.

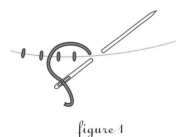

figure 1

AT THE FINISH LINE

Before you start any hand stitch, tie a knot at the end of the thread. When you finish the seam, make a few stitches in the same place to secure the thread, then snip off any excess.

BACKSTITCH

The backstitch is a basic hand-stitching method for creating a seam (figure 2). It's good for holding seams under pressure or to outline shapes or text.

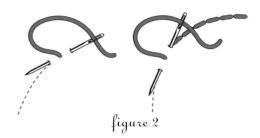

figure 2

BASTING STITCH

Basting is a way to temporarily secure two edges of fabric where a seam will go. The basting stitch is the same as a running stitch (figure 5). You just make it with very long stitches you can remove more easily once the permanent stitch is in place.

BLANKET STITCH

The blanket stitch is a decorative and functional technique you can use to accentuate an edge or attach a cut shape to a layer of fabric (figure 3).

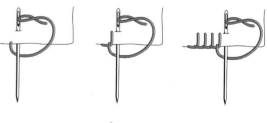

figure 3

CHAIN STITCH

The chain stitch, or "Lazy Daisy stitch," can be worked in a circle to form a flower (figure 4).

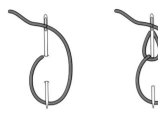

figure 4

RUNNING STITCH

You create this stitch by weaving the needle through the fabric at evenly spaced intervals (figure 5).

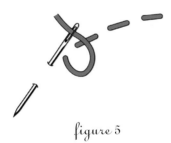

figure 5

SLIPSTITCH

The slipstitch is also a good stitch for closing up seams. Slip the needle through one end of the open seam to anchor the thread, then take a small stitch through the fold and pull the needle through. In the other piece of fabric, insert the needle directly opposite the stitch you just made, and take a stitch through the fold. Keep going until you're done (figure 6).

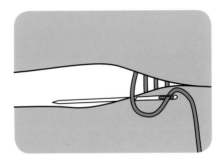

figure 6

WHIPSTITCH

The whipstitch (also called an overcast stitch) is used to bind edges to prevent raveling. Sew the stitches over the edge of the fabric (figure 7).

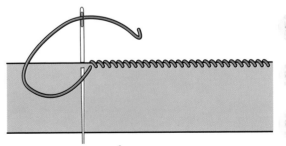

figure 7

householdhelp

Useful and beautiful—
what more could you want
from these patchwork pieces?

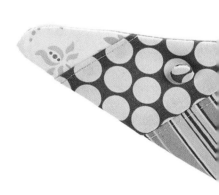

a patchwork orange pocket quilt

*T*his nifty hanging quilt has six squares that act as pockets—perfect for stashing letters, trinkets, keys, glasses, or anything else you don't want left hanging around. Orange you ready to get organized?

WHAT YOU NEED

Basic Patchwork Tool Kit (page 11)

½ yard (45.7 cm) plaid cotton for background

15 x 17-inch (38.1 x 43.2 cm) piece of felt

Thread in a complementary color

Package of ½-inch (1.3 cm) double-fold bias tape for the border

¼ yard (22.9 cm) each of 5 assorted cotton fabrics for the pocket squares

18-inch dowel or bamboo stick, ⅜ inch in diameter

SEAM ALLOWANCE

Varies

DESIGNER

JOAN K. MORRIS

WHAT YOU DO

1 Cut out two 17 x 18-inch (43.2 x 45.7 cm) pieces of the plaid cotton. Place the felt on the back of one of the cut pieces, aligned at the bottom. It will be 3 inches (7.6 cm) shorter than the top. Place the remaining plaid piece right sides together, and pin the edges.

2 Using a ½-inch (1.3 cm) seam allowance, machine stitch all the way around in from the edge, leaving a 3-inch (7.6 cm) opening. Clip the corners, and turn the piece right side out. (The top edge is the one where the felt does not reach the edge.) Press. Hand stitch the opening closed.

3 Add decorative bias tape by opening the tape and folding one end. Then place the tape in position, with the raw edge lined up with the edge of the quilt. Stitch ½ inch (1.3 cm)

in from the edge. Fold the tape to the back of the piece, and hand stitch in place.

4 Fold the top edge over so the piece is 16 inches (40.6 cm) tall, creating a sleeve in the top for the dowel to fit into. Hand stitch this in place. Set the background aside.

5 Using figure 1 as a guide, cut the appropriate number of squares and triangles from each fabric. The following pieces will make one 4½-inch (11.4 cm) square pocket (seam allowances are included throughout):

figure 1

- The four center squares are 1¾ inches (4.4 cm) each.

- The four smaller triangles are made from 3¼-inch (8.3 cm) squares cut in half diagonally.

- The four larger triangles are made from 4¼-inch (10.8 cm) squares cut in half diagonally.

To make all six pockets, you will need six times as many of the shapes shown in the figure.

6 To assemble the squares, start with the center. Machine stitch two squares together with a ¼-inch (0.6 cm) seam allowance and then the other two. Press the seams open. Then stitch the two pairs together, and press the seams open again.

7 Place one of the smaller triangles on one of the edges of the square with the points overlapping the edge (figure 2). Machine stitch the edge of the triangle and the square. Press this seam into the center. Stitch another triangle on the opposite side the same way. Now stitch the remaining two triangles to the other sides with the edges extending over the points of the first triangles. Press all the seams to the center. Carefully clip off any points that remain.

figure 2

8 Attach the larger triangles in the same way. If the edges aren't even, make the pieces square with the rotary cutter. Do this after you've completed all the squares so they are all the same size.

9 Repeat steps 6, 7, and 8 until you have six squares.

10 Place three of the squares side by side, and arrange them with the colors alternating. Machine stitch them together in a row with a ¼-inch (0.6 cm) seam allowance. Be sure to match the points. Repeat with the other three.

11 Measure the sewn strips of squares, and cut two pieces of the plaid cotton to this measurement. Place a piece of the cut plaid right sides together with the strip of squares and pin. Machine stitch ¼ inch (0.6 cm) in from the edge all the way around, and leave a 3-inch (7.6 cm) opening. Clip the corners, turn right side out, and press. Fold and press the opening, and hand stitch closed. Repeat with the other strip.

12 Place the pieces in position on the background. Leave a 3-inch (7.6 cm) gap between the two rows of pockets. Pin in place, and machine stitch close to the edge around the sides and bottom of the pocket. Then machine stitch between each square to create three pockets per strip. Place the dowel in position.

*starlet*pincushion

You'll be seeing stars when you stick your pins in this darling pincushion. With simple variations on fabric, the sky's the limit.

DESIGNER

DORIE BLAISDELL SCHWARZ

WHAT YOU NEED

Basic Patchwork Tool Kit (page 11)

⅛ yard (11.4 cm) cotton fabric A or scraps

⅛ yard (11.4 cm) cotton fabric B or scraps

Thread to match

6-inch (15.2 cm) square of wool felt

2½ x 14-inch (6.4 x 35.6 cm) strip cotton fabric C

Stuffing (wool or your choice)

SEAM ALLOWANCE

¼ inch (0.6 cm)

WHAT YOU DO

1 Cut six of template A from fabric A. (See page 123 for all templates in this project.) Cut six of template B from fabric B. On the wrong side of the fabric, mark a line ¼ inch (0.6 cm) from all edges of all the A pieces for your sewing line. Do the same on the two angled sides of the B pieces.

2 To sew the top, match up two A pieces with right sides facing. Stitching on the sewing line, sew the two pieces together on just one of the four sides. Make sure to back-tack when starting and ending the seam, and start and finish at the angles as accurately as possible.

3 With wrong sides facing, open up the work, and finger press the seam to the right. Turn the work over to the front side, and add another piece A to the right-hand edge of the right piece A. Sew the seam as you did for the previous seam. Continue to add A pieces until all six have been chained together. Then close the star by stitching the first to the last.

4 On the back of the star, the center will look clumpy. Make sure you have all the seams going in the same direction (figure 1). Then use your finger to find the center of the clump, and press down. The tiny center points will fan out in a circle. Press.

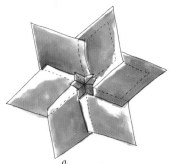

figure 1

5 Line up the point of a piece B in the crevice between two A pieces, front sides facing. The point of the stitching line of piece B should match the intersection of the stitching lines of A (figure 2). Sew piece B to the star using two separate seams, one from the point of the first A to the point of B and the other from the point of B to the point of the second A. Stay on the stitching lines, and back-tack at the start and end.

figure 2

6 Repeat with five other B pieces. Press flat. You'll need to neaten the resulting hexagon with messy edges. Use a ruler to make a line 1/4 inch (0.6 cm) greater than the distance from hexagon point to hexagon point. Trim the hexagon on this line.

7 All your hexagon sides probably won't be exactly the same, so use the top as a template to cut a hexagon shape from the felt to be used for the bottom of the pincushion. Put the top on the felt, right sides facing. Carefully cut around the hexagon. To mark corresponding sides, put one pin in one side of the top and one pin in the same side of the felt. Put the felt bottom aside.

8 With right sides facing, line up strip C with the side of the top that has the pin on it. Stitch C to the top, starting in the middle of the pin side of the hexagon and 1/2 inch (1.3 cm) from the end of C. Stitch all around the top, stopping, lifting the foot, and turning the fabric at the corners. When you reach the start, back-tack and clip the threads. Close C by sewing a seam perpendicular to the hexagon top. Clip any extra C down to 1/2 inch (1.3 cm).

9 With right sides facing, sew the felt bottom to C on five sides. Turn and stuff until plump, but don't push your seams too hard. Hand stitch the opening closed.

home*sweet*home
coasters

*P*rotect your coffee table in style with these down-home coasters. Made from felt and fabric remnants, these coasters can be pieced together in a flash.

DESIGNER
WENDY ARACICH

WHAT YOU NEED

Basic Patchwork Tool Kit (page 11)

Remnants of three coordinating fabrics

Thread

1/4 yard (22.9 cm) wool felt

Utility knife

Embroidery floss

Embroidery needle

SEAM ALLOWANCE

1/4 inch (0.6 cm)

WHAT YOU DO

1 Cut 3 1/2 x 1-inch (8.9 x 2.5 cm) rectangular strips from the coordinating fabrics for a total of 64 strips. Cut eight 4 3/4 x 4 3/4-inch (12 x 12 cm) squares of felt.

2 Arrange strips vertically (longer sides together) into eight rows of eight rectangular strips. Join strips one row at a time, starting by pinning the right edge of the first strip to the left edge of the second strip, with right sides together. Next, pin the right edge of the second strip to the left edge of the third strip. Repeat until all strips in a row are pinned. Set aside, and repeat with the remaining rows.

3 Machine stitch along the pinned edges. Press seams open.

4 Pair stitched rows, and stitch the bottom of the top row to the top of the bottom row. Repeat with remaining rows to make a total of four pairs. Machine stitch along pinned edges. Press seams open.

5 On the wrong side of four pieces of felt, center the template (see the template on page 120) and trace with the pencil. Using the rotary cutter or a utility knife, cut out shapes carefully along the traced lines, and take care not to cut through the area outside of the traced line.

6 Pin patchwork, right side up, to the underside of the cut felt. Adjust the placement of the felt to compose your patchwork within the house shape. Don't worry if the patchwork extends beyond the sides of the coasters.

7 With the embroidery floss, sew a running stitch around the perimeter of the house shapes, 1/4 inch (0.6 cm) from the edge, and take care to catch the patchwork with the stitches. Turn the coaster over, and carefully trim the patchwork about 1/2 inch (1.3 cm) outside the stitches.

8 Pin the coaster back to the front, wrong sides together. Machine stitch around the perimeter. Repeat with the remaining coasters.

hugs and kisses card

$\mathcal{M}$ake a one-of-a-kind card for someone special. All it takes is some card stock, fabric scraps, and a little bit of time. P.S. Don't forget the stamp!

DESIGNER

WENDI GRATZ

WHAT YOU NEED

Basic Patchwork Tool Kit (page 11)

Scraps of fabric, two colors

Thread, complementary with your darker color

Square ruler

2 pieces of 8½ x 11-inch (21.6 x 27.9 cm) white card stock

Acid-free glue stick

SEAM ALLOWANCE

¼ inch (0.6 cm)

WHAT YOU DO

1 Cut five squares 1¾ x 1¾ inches (4.4 x 4.4 cm) from the first color. (On the card pictured, it's the red fabric.) Cut 10 strips about 1 x 2 inches (2.5 x 5.1 cm) from the second color (here, the green). Cut 10 more strips about 1 x 3½ inches (2.5 x 8.9 cm) from the second color.

2 Lay one square and one shorter strip right sides together and stitch. Repeat with the remaining squares. Press all seams flat. Now add a second shorter strip to the opposite side of each square, and press seams flat.

3 Trim up the strip edges to match the edges of the squares. Attach the longer strips to the remaining sides of the squares. You should have five squares surrounded by strips.

4 Crop each block to a 2-inch (5.1 cm) square with the square of the first color roughly centered and set at an angle inside the square of the second color. Here's how to do it:

- Lay your transparent square ruler down onto one of the fabric blocks so that the central 1-inch (2.5 cm) square is roughly centered inside a 2½-inch (6.4 cm) square formed by two edges of the ruler.

- Turn the ruler a little to set the central square at an angle within the 2½-inch (6.4 cm) square (as shown in figure 1).

- With your rotary cutter, trim the block on the two sides of the ruler. Turn the block under the ruler to align the two trimmed edges with the 2½-inch (6.4 cm) markings on the ruler sides. Trim the other two sides of the square.

- Repeat with the other blocks.

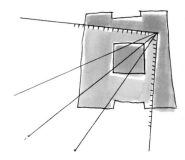

figure 1

5 Cut a 5 x 10-inch (12.7 x 25.4 cm) rectangle from the card stock, and fold it in half for your card. Trace the envelope pattern (see the template on page 122) onto the remaining piece of card stock. Cut it out. Fold in the short side tabs first, then the short bottom flap, then the long top flap.

6 Lay out four of the patchwork blocks on the card and one on the top flap of your envelope. With a dab of the glue stick in the center of each block, attach the blocks to the card stock.

7 Stitch close to the edge of each patchwork block all the way around the blocks. Trim away the thread tails. With the glue stick, attach the bottom flap of the envelope to the tabs on the sides. When it's time to mail the card, you'll need to seal the envelope with the glue stick.

spiffypotholders

DESIGNER

WENDY ARACICH

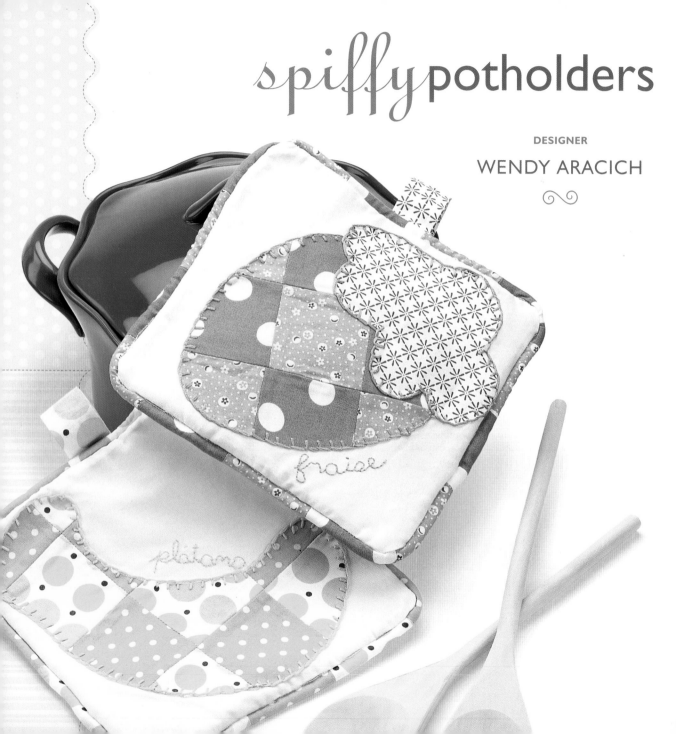

*C*an't take the heat? Stitch up these fun, vintage-inspired potholders to add some pizzazz to your kitchen. Embroidered blanket-stitching and patchwork piping add an extra dash of adorable.

WHAT YOU NEED

Basic Patchwork Tool Kit (page 11)

¼ yard (22.9 cm) or a fat quarter each of four fabrics (two shades of pink and two of yellow)

¼ yard (22.9 cm) white cotton

White thread

Remnant green fabric

⅛ yard (11.4 cm) paper-backed fusible web

Pink and yellow embroidery floss

Embroidery needle

2 yards (1.8 m) of cord for piping

¼ yard (22.9 cm) insulated batting

SEAM ALLOWANCE

¼ inch (0.6 cm)

WHAT YOU DO

1 Cut ten 2½-inch (6.4 cm) squares of each yellow fabric for a total of 20 yellow squares. Cut nine 2½-inch (6.4 cm) squares of light pink fabric and eight 2½-inch (6.4 cm) squares of dark pink fabric for a total of 17 pink squares. Cut four 7½ x 7½-inch (19 x 19 cm) squares of white cotton. Cut two 7½ x 7½-inch (19 x 19 cm) squares of insulated batting.

2 Arrange the 2½-inch (6.4 cm) squares on a work surface, yellow in three columns and four rows and pink in three columns and three rows. Arrange the squares in an "every other" pattern with an equal amount of each fabric. Set aside the remaining 16 squares (eight yellow and eight pink).

3 For each grouping of squares, beginning with the first row, pin the right edge of the first square to the left edge of the second square with right sides together. Next, pin the right edge of the second square to the left edge of the third square. Set aside, and repeat with remaining rows.

4 Machine stitch along pinned edges. Press seams open. For each grouping of squares, join rows from top to bottom along common edges, and be sure to match seams. Press seams open.

5 On the wrong side of the fabric, trace the banana template on yellow patchwork and the strawberry template on pink patchwork. Trace the strawberry leaf template on green fabric (see the templates on page 121). Adjust the template placement to determine composition of patchwork within the shape. Cut out the shapes carefully along the traced lines.

6 Pin the fruit shapes to the fusible web, right side up, and slowly cut out. Remove pins, and iron fabric to web following the manufacturer's instructions.

7 Remove the strawberry's paper backing, and place the strawberry where you wish on white fabric, right side up. Iron to fuse the strawberry to the white fabric. Then place the leaf where you wish on top of the strawberry and white fabric, and iron to fuse. Repeat with the banana on a separate piece of white fabric.

8 With the pink embroidery floss, sew a blanket stitch around the perimeter of the strawberry and leaf. With the yellow embroidery floss, sew a blanket stitch around the perimeter of the banana. Then

using embroidery floss and a simple backstitch, freehand "fraise" on the strawberry potholder and "platano" on the banana.

9 Arrange the remaining squares in two rows, one of pinks and one of yellows, in an "every other" pattern. Working from left to right, seam together squares to form rows. Press seams open. Then cut each row in half lengthwise. Pin two strips together end to end, and stitch to create a longer strip. Press seams open. Repeat with the other row.

10 Cut two 32-inch (80 cm) pieces of piping cord. Lay on top of the patchwork rows, right side down, and center the cord (figure 1). Fold in half, wrong sides together. Pin along the inside of the cord and stitch.

11 Align the raw edge of the piping with the edge of the potholder front, and pin

along the stitched line, curving the piping at the corners and overlapping at ends; trim away any excess cord if necessary before you overlap the ends. Stitch along the seamline.

12 Cut two 2½ x 4½ (6.4 x 11.4 cm) pieces of coordinating fabric, one for each potholder. Fold in half, right sides together, and sew. Turn right side out and press. Then pin a loop to the right side of the potholder front, aligning the raw edge with the top center of the potholder. Stitch or baste in place.

13 For each potholder, layer the following from bottom to top in this order: insulated batting, backing fabric (right side up), and potholder front (right side down). Pin carefully along previously sewn line, and be sure to catch all layers and leave a 2-inch (5.1 cm) opening at the bottom of the potholder. Stitch. Then turn potholders right side out and press. Stitch opening closed by hand.

figure 1

treehouse place mats

Setting the table is never a chore with these funky decorative place mats. Branch out your dining decor with a subtle tree design in crisp embroidered linen and assorted earthy patterns.

DESIGNER

JOAN K. MORRIS

WHAT YOU NEED

Basic Patchwork Tool Kit (page 11)

Scrap paper

¼ yard (22.9 cm) blue and green striped blend fabric

¼ yard (22.9 cm) blue linen fabric

Paper-backed fusible web

¼ yard (22.9 cm) brown paisley cotton fabric

Matching thread

Invisible thread

½ yard (45.7 cm) embroidered fabric with cream background and blue and green embroidery

13 x 18-inch (33 x 45.7 cm) piece of felt or thick interfacing for each place mat

Knitting needle

SEAM ALLOWANCE

¼ inch (0.6 cm)

WHAT YOU DO

1 Cut out a 13 x 18-inch (33 x 45.7 cm) piece of scrap paper. Measure 1/2 inch (1.3 cm) in from the edge, and draw a line for the seam allowance. Draw your own design inside the lines.

2 Measure the rectangles on your design, and add 1/2 inch (1.3 cm) to the length and width of each for a 1/4-inch (0.6 cm) seam allowance. Cut the fabric to these measurements. Cut the horizontal pieces of the striped fabric the same length as the centerpiece rectangle by 1 1/2 inches (3.8 cm) wide. Cut the vertical striped pieces to the length of the blue linen fabric plus the length of the striped pieces (plus the 1/2 inch [1.3 cm] for the seam allowance) by 1 1/2 inches (3.8 cm) wide. Measure and cut the brown paisley strips and the blue linen strips in a similar fashion, making these pieces wider as desired.

3 Following the manufacturer's instructions, adhere the fusible web to the back of a piece of the brown paisley cotton big enough to cover the size of the tree. Then cut out the tree design from your first drawing, or trace the shape onto scrap paper and cut it out. On the brown fabric, draw around the cutout of the tree.

4 Cut the tree out of the brown fabric. Remove the paper backing, and iron the tree in place on the right side of the center rectangle of fabric. Iron the fusible web onto the back of a piece of the striped fabric large enough to make the eight circles on the tree. Draw the circles on the paper backing, and cut them out. Then remove the backing, position the circles on the tree, and iron in place.

5 With invisible thread in the top of the sewing machine and regular thread in the bobbin, zigzag around the whole edge of the tree and circles. Then stitch the horizontal pieces of the striped fabric to the top and bottom of the appliquéd piece with a 1/4-inch (0.6 cm) seam allowance. Press the seams open.

6 Machine stitch the vertical pieces of the striped fabric to the sides of the appliquéd fabric. This should be a rectangle. Press the seams open.

7 Stitch the horizontal brown pieces to the top and bottom, and do the same with the last fabric strips. Then machine stitch the embroidered fabric to the sides of the tree piece, placing the larger piece to the right. Press the seams open.

8 Cut a piece of the felt and a piece of the embroidered fabric to the same measurement as the sewn piece.

9 Place the cut felt on the back of the sewn piece. Place the cut piece of the embroidered fabric right sides together with the tree piece. Pin in place. Machine stitch 1/2 inch (1.3 cm) from the edge all the way around, and leave a 3-inch (7.6 cm) opening. Clip the corners, and trim any excess felt or fabric.

10 Turn the place mat right side out through the 3-inch (7.6 cm) hole. Push out the corner with the knitting needle. Press flat, and fold and press the opening. Hand stitch the opening closed.

11 For the binding, cut two pieces of the blue fabric 2 inches (5.1 cm) wide by the length of the sides plus 2 inches (5.1 cm). Place and pin the blue pieces to the edge of the place mat with right sides together and raw edges aligned. Machine stitch ½ inch (1.3 cm) from the edge.

12 Fold and press the binding pieces to the back, folding the excess under to create a finished edge. Hand stitch the binding to the backside.

REVERSE IT FIRST

When you transfer your cut-out tree pattern to the iron-on material, the process will reverse the image. To keep the final tree looking the same as your original design, just flip over the paper image you've cut out.

executive chef apron

*I*t's time to cut out the apron strings and have some fun. Here, a basic apron is transformed with patchwork detailing and a savvy little wool pocket.

DESIGNER

RUTH SINGER

WHAT YOU NEED

Basic Patchwork Tool Kit (page 11)

Piece 1, wool, 11 x 6 inches
(27.9 x 15.2 cm)

Piece 2, patterned, 6 x 13 inches
(15.2 x 33 cm)

Piece 3, main fabric, 8 x 4 inches
(20.3 x 10.2 cm)

Piece 4, wool, 8 x 4 inches
(20.3 x 10.2 cm)

Piece 5, patterned, 13 x 5
(33 x 12.7 cm)

Rickrack, 3 yards (2.7 m)

Basting thread

Green fabric

Pocket facing, patterned,
5 x 2 inches (12.7 x 5.1 cm)

Pocket main fabric, wool,
6½ x 8 inches (16.5 x 20.3 cm)

Green thread

Main fabric, 25 x 18 inches
(63.5 x 45.7 cm)

Lining in coordinating color,
40 x 18 inches (101.6 x 45.7 cm)

Knitting needle or blunt pencil

Thread in complementary colors

1½-inch (3.8 cm) grosgrain
ribbon, 1½ yards (1.3 m)

SEAM ALLOWANCE

¼ inch (0.6 cm)

WHAT YOU DO

1 Make the patchwork panels. Cut one each of pieces 1 to 5 with the pattern face up. Then cut one each of pieces 1 to 5 with the pattern face down, so you have panels for the left and right side of the apron. Be sure you match the grain lines marked on the pattern. Mark each piece with its number, the right side of the fabric, the sewing lines, and whether it is left or right side.

2 Sew on the rickrack following this method: cut lengths of rickrack to match the wiggly line markings on pattern pieces 2 and 4; baste the rickrack centered over the sewing lines on these pieces on the front side of the fabric.

3 Place together pieces 1 and 2, and match the sewing lines up. Put the right sides together so the rickrack is in the middle of the sandwich. Sew along the seam next to the basting stitches, and remove the basting. Sew piece 3 onto piece 2 in the same way, and continue until you have all five pieces joined.

4 Remove all the basting, and trim the seam allowances to ⅜ inch (1 cm). Press the seam allowances open, turn the piece over, and press the rickrack to the correct side.

5 Place the side panel pattern piece over the sewn panel, and trim to size. Make the other side in the same way.

6 Make the pocket. Cut the pocket piece from green fabric, and mark the pleating lines. Overcast or serge the curved edges to stop fraying. Make the pleat by folding the arrows to the center line (figure 1). Baste in place at the top edge only. Place the facing piece right side down on the pocket piece, and match the top edges. Stitch the two pieces together using a ⅝-inch

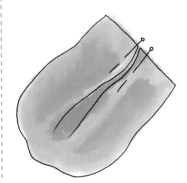

figure 1

(1.6 cm) seam allowance. Remove the pleat basting stitches. From the reverse side, press the seam allowances up toward the facing. All around the pocket, including the facing, turn under and press a 1/2-inch (1.3 cm) seam allowance on the reverse side. Fold the facing over onto the reverse side of the pocket, and topstitch the facing in place.

7 Cut the main fabric panel, and place the pattern piece on the fold of the fabric. Mark the sewing lines along the side seams, and baste the rickrack in place as before. Position the pocket as you wish; you can use the photo here as a general guide. Stitch around the pocket with the matching thread about 1/4 inch (0.6 cm) from the folded edge. Be sure you don't sew up the opening.

8 Sew the side panels onto the main fabric with the right sides together. Use the basting as your sewing guide. Remove the basting, and press the seam allowances open. Turn over, and press the rickrack onto the main fabric side.

9 Use your complete apron panel as a pattern to cut the lining, following the grain of the main skirt piece. With the wrong side up, fold and press 1/2 inch (1.3 cm) along the top edge. Do the same with the apron piece, again folding the seam allowance onto the back side of the panel.

10 Place the lining and apron right sides together, and sew around the sides and bottom hem with a 5/8-inch (1.6 cm) seam allowances. Trim the seam allowances to 3/8 inch (1 cm).

11 Turn the apron the right way around, and carefully turn out the corners with the knitting needle. Press all the edges flat so the lining can't be seen from the front.

12 Next, apply the ribbon waistband. Measure the center of the apron panel, mark with a pin, and match the center of the ribbon. The top edge of the ribbon should be along the folded-under top edges of the apron. Pin in place, and machine stitch close to the edge of the ribbon along the top edge, the sides of the apron, and the bottom of the ribbon. Try it on, and adjust the length of the ribbon ties if needed.

*spa*sachets

Relax after a stressful day with soothing lavender eye
pillows that are easy to make and smell heavenly.

DESIGNER

BELINDA ANDRESSON

WHAT YOU NEED

Basic Patchwork Tool Kit (page 11)

7 pieces of several different prints, at least 2 x 5 inches (5.1 x 12.7 cm) and a 4½-inch (11.4 cm) square

Thread

¼-inch (0.6 cm) foot (optional)

Chopstick

25 g of lavender per sachet

Funnel

SEAM ALLOWANCE

¼ inch (0.6 cm)

REJUVENATE YOURSELF

For an home spa experience, pop one of these beauties in the microwave for a few seconds, or chill in the refrigerator, and place it on your tired eyes or forehead.

WHAT YOU DO

1. Select your fabric from either a charm pack of 6-inch (15.2 cm) squares or scraps left over from previous projects.

2. With the rotary cutter, cut a 2-inch (5.1 cm) square, five or six 1½-inch-wide (3.8 cm) strips, and one or two strips 1 or 2 inches (2.5 or 5.1 cm) wide. Cut a 4½-inch (11.4 cm) square for the back of your sachet.

3. Starting with the center 2-inch (5.1 cm) square, begin building outward, first with the top piece and moving clockwise (figure 1). After sewing each piece, iron seams flat and trim the excess so the patchwork is square.

4. Continue building the patchwork until the center square is framed by strips on each of the four sides. Next, measure your patchwork, which should be 4½ inches (11.4 cm) square. Add more strips if needed.

figure 1

5. With right sides together, join the front patchwork to the back. Leave a 2-inch (5.1 cm) opening on one side, and stitch around the square. Backstitch at the beginning and end of the opening to secure the stitches. Clip the corners, and press seams at the opening back.

6. Turn right side out through the opening. Push out corners using a chopstick; then press the piece flat. Using the funnel, fill with lavender. Once filled, stitch the opening closed with a slipstitch.

FUN WITH FUNNELS

Don't have a funnel? You can fashion your own by cutting a plastic water bottle in half (one with a regular-size opening, not a wide one) and drying the inside thoroughly.

outside the box

*T*hink outside the box with these soft storage containers. They're perfect for stashing sewing supplies, bathroom essentials, and anything else that needs a little home.

DESIGNER

AIMEE RAY

WHAT YOU NEED

Basic Patchwork Tool Kit (page 11)

Several patterned fabrics of different colors

Colored embroidery floss

SEAM ALLOWANCE

¼ inch (0.6 cm)

WHAT YOU DO

1 Cut 2-inch (5.1 cm) squares from the fabrics. You will need six squares for each rectangle and four for each square. Sew the 2-inch (5.1 cm) squares together using ¼-inch (0.6 cm) seams to form larger squares or rectangles for the sides. All measurements in the project include seam allowances.

2 For the horizontal box, cut two 3¼ x 4½-inch (8.3 x 11.4 cm) patchwork rectangles, two 3¼-inch (8.3 cm) patchwork squares for the sides, two

3¼-inch (8.3 cm) fabric squares, and four fabric rectangles for the lining and bottoms.

3 For the vertical box, cut four 3¼ x 4½-inch (8.3 x 11.4 cm) patchwork rectangles for the sides, four fabric rectangles for the lining, and two 3¼-inch (8.3 cm) fabric squares for the bottoms.

4 For each box, sew the four patchwork pieces together at the sides with a ¼-inch (0.6 cm) seam to form the box shape, using either a fabric square or a rectangle for the bottom. Sew together the remaining fabric pieces to make another box the same size and shape for the lining. Leave half of one side open at the bottom of the lining.

5 Turn the patchwork piece right side out and the lining inside out. Fit the patchwork piece inside the lining, and line up the top edges. Pin them together, and sew around the edge (figure 1).

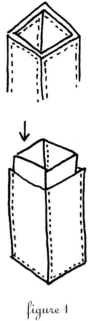

figure 1

6 Turn the piece right side out through the open hole in the lining, and then sew the hole closed. Push the lining down inside the outer box. Press the corners and top edge of the box.

7 With the embroidery floss, stitch a decorative line of embroidery—such as the blanket stitch, chain stitch, and running stitch—along the top edge of each box.

hanger**with**care

Special clothes deserve special treatment, and this patchwork design will pamper your best threads. For intimate apparel and garments with straps, the button detailing acts as a clever non-slip device.

DESIGNER

VALERIE SHRADER

WHAT YOU NEED

Basic Patchwork Tool Kit (page 11)

Fabric for patchwork, 1/8 yard (11.4 cm) of 6 different prints

Coordinating sewing thread

Wire hanger

Fabric for back, 1/4 yard (22.9 cm) of a solid color

Coordinating decorative, variegated rayon thread

2 half-ball covered buttons, 7/16 (1.1 cm) in diameter

SEAM ALLOWANCE

1/4 inch (0.6 cm)

WHAT YOU DO

1 Cut seven 3 x 9-inch (7.6 x 22.9 cm) strips of fabric with the rotary cutter. If desired, trim a couple of the strips to 2 x 9 inches (5.1 x 22.9 cm). Lay out the strips (each in a vertical position) from left to right on your work surface in the order you'd like in the final piece. Start with the left piece and use the strip-piecing method (see page 20) to assemble the strips together. The final pieced block should be at least 9 x 16 inches (22.9 x 40.6 cm). Press the seams to one side.

2 Place the hanger on the patchwork so the strips flow on the diagonal, and trace around it, adding a ¼-inch (0.6 cm) seam allowance. Cut out the cover. Using the patchwork piece as a guide, cut an identical backing piece from the solid fabric.

3 With the decorative thread, topstitch along one side of each seam of the patchwork.

4 With the right sides together, pin the back to the front, and leave most of the bottom open. Stitch, beginning and ending on the bottom, 1 inch (2.5 cm) around the corner. Leave a 1-inch (2.5 cm) opening at the top through which to slide the hanger neck. Notch the curves (figure 1).

5 Turn and press the open edges under. Slide the hanger into the cover, beginning with the neck, and slipstitch the bottom closed. To make it easier to stitch, pull the edges together under the hanger bottom and pin.

6 If desired, add the covered buttons to prevent delicate straps from sliding off the hanger. Place buttons at the upper edge.

figure 1

hold it right here

Bring along one of these bags and carriers to hold essential items in classic style.

scraptopcover

*A*ll work and no play? Achieve the right balance with this pretty and protective laptop cover. When it's time to call it a day, your computer will sleep sounder than ever.

DESIGNER

BRIDGET M. GOSS

54

WHAT YOU NEED

Basic Patchwork Tool Kit (page 11)

½ yard (45.7 cm) print fabric A (for gusset and middle patchwork panel)

¼ yard (22.9 cm) assorted complementary fabrics B (for left and right patchwork panels)

½ yard (45.7 cm) fabric C (for lining)

½ yard (45.7 cm) paisley fabric D (for cover back and for patchwork)

Thread in a complementary color

Fusible batting, at least 1 yard

Zipper, 18 inches (45.7 cm), in a complementary color to print fabric A

SEAM ALLOWANCE

½ inch (1.3 cm)

WHAT YOU DO

1 Measure the length (L), width (W), and depth (D) of your laptop computer. ("L" here is the distance across when facing the computer as it is used. "D" is how deep it is when closed.) Add ½ inch (1.3 cm) to both the L and W measurements. This is your "finished cover" measurement. To allow for seam allowances, add 1 more inch (2.5 cm) to the L and W in your finished cover measurement. This is your "pre-sewn cover" measurement.

MAKE THE PATCHWORK TOP:

2 You'll construct three panels of a similar size.

For the middle panel: Cut a piece of the print fabric A that is slightly bigger than one-third the length (L) by the width (W) of your pre-sewn cover measurement from step 1.

For the two side panels: Piece together two patchwork panels that are the same dimensions as the middle panel. To do so, cut pieces from the assorted fabrics B to lay out in strips and squares, using the photo on the facing page as a guide. Stitch together with the strip-piecing method described on page 20. (You can make the rectangles slightly oversize and trim them later.) Press the seams.

3 Arrange the panels and stitch together with the right sides together. Press all seams. Trim the entire piece to the pre-sewn cover measurements from step 1.

CUT THE BACK COVER AND LINING PIECES:

4 Cut three pieces of the lining fabric C to the pre-sewn cover measurement from step 1. You will use two of these pieces for the lining and the remaining one for the back of the cover.

DO THE MATH

Here's a typical example of the measurements required in step 1. The instructions will refer to these dimensions as examples throughout.

Laptop
L x W x D = 14 x 10½ x 1¾ inches (35.6 x 26.7 x 4.4 cm)

Finished cover
L x W = 14½ x 11 inches (36.8 x 27.9 cm)

Pre-sewn cover
L x W = 15½ x 12 inches (38.1 x 30.5 cm)

CUT THE GUSSET AND GUSSET LINING PIECES:

5 To figure the appropriate dimensions for your laptop, add the following:

- your "D" measurement from step 1
- ¼ inch (0.6 cm) for ease
- 1 inch (2.5 cm) for seam allowance
- the thickness of the batting

Using the example from the "Do the Math" box, if you are using batting ¼ inch (0.6 cm) thick, the gusset depth would be determined as follows:

1¾ inches (4.4 cm) + ¼ inch (0.6 cm) + 1 inch (2.5 cm) + ¼ inch (0.6 cm) = 3¼ inches (8.3 cm)

6 Cut one strip of print fabric A to the measurement from step 5 and to the length of one-half of the perimeter of the finished cover measurement from step 1, plus 1 inch for the seam allowance.

Using the example from the "Do the Math" box, you would cut the gusset strips to 3¼ x 26½ inches. Repeat to cut a second strip of identical size from lining fabric C.

7 Cut one more strip from the print fabric A and one more strip from the lining fabric C that are the same dimensions as those cut in step 6, but add one additional inch (2.5 cm) to the depth. You will need this additional inch for the seam allowance for the centered zipper you will install in step 11. Cut these pieces in half lengthwise.

Continuing with the example from step 6, these strips would be 4¼ x 26½ inches before being cut in half.

CUT AND FUSE THE BATTING:

8 To protect your laptop, you will apply fusible batting to every piece of the cover and the lining. For the fronts and backs of the cover and the lining, cut four pieces of batting to your finished cover measurement from step 1.

9 For the gusset and gusset lining, cut four pieces of batting that are the same measurement as the depth you figured in step 5, minus the 1-inch seam allowance, by the length you figured in step 6, minus the additional 1-inch seam allowance. Cut two of these pieces in half lengthwise.

Using the same examples used in steps 5 and 6, the batting for the gusset and its lining would be cut to 2¼ x 25½ inches.

10 Following the manufacturer's instructions, fuse each piece of the batting to its respective fabric piece; the "half" pieces of batting are fused to the gusset and gusset lining pieces that were cut in half.

INSTALL THE ZIPPER AND STITCH THE GUSSET:

11 Use the fabric A gusset strips that were cut in half to install a centered zipper. (As a refresher, a centered zipper is installed between two pieces of fabric that are stitched together at either end of the zipper opening, and the zipper is placed in between. Sew in place with a zipper foot.)

12 Sew the remaining fabric A gusset strip to the zipper portion at the short ends, right sides together, to form a continuous band.

CONSTRUCT THE COVER:

13 With right sides facing, pin the zipper gusset to the patchwork front cover, placing the seams in the gusset at the midpoints of the short sides of the cover (figure 1). (Be sure to orient the zipper across the top of your patchwork cover, and not the bottom.) Pin securely and/or hand baste before stitching to keep the gusset in place while you sew. Stitch, pivoting at the corners and clipping the gusset as necessary. You may find it helpful to mark the corners on the gusset before you sew.

figure 1

14 Unzip the zipper and repeat step 13 to sew the back cover to the zipper gusset. Turn right-side out through the open zipper.

CONSTRUCT THE LINING:

15 To make the gusset lining, use the two halved pieces to replicate the piece you made to install the zipper in step 11; it should have a center opening of the identical length. Press the seams open along the entire length, including the center opening. Stitch this piece to the remaining gusset lining strip at the short ends, right sides together, to form a continuous band as in step 12.

16 Sew the gusset lining to the lining front and back pieces as in step 13.

17 Insert the lining into the cover, with the wrong sides facing. Hand-stitch the lining to the cover along the zipper tape.

perky bird coffee jacket

𝒯oo hot to handle? Make one of these cool coffee sleeves and you'll be sipping your latte in style. A thin inner layer of batting provides enough protection to make it completely cozy.

WHAT YOU NEED

Basic Patchwork Tool Kit (page 11)

Thin polyester batting, 8 x 8 inches (20.3 x 20.3 cm)

2 coordinating scraps of fabric, each at least 8 inches (20.3 cm) square

Scrap of contrasting fabric, 2 x 2 inches (5.1 x 5.1 cm)

Contrasting thread

SEAM ALLOWANCE

¼ inch (0.6 cm)

DESIGNER

SHANNON UDELL

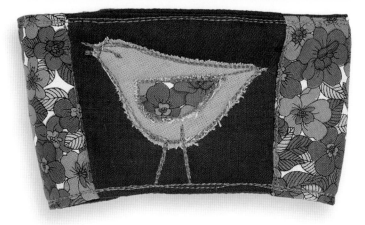

WHAT YOU DO

1 Trace the templates (see page 122) onto paper, and cut them out. Cutting measurements include a ¼-inch (0.6 cm) seam allowance. Follow this list:

- Cut 4 of the sleeve pattern from the batting

- Cut 6 of the sleeve pattern from the fabric you want for lining (4 will be used for lining and 2 for the outside)

- Cut 2 of the sleeve pattern from the coordinating fabric for the outside

- Cut a wing shape from the coordinating fabric

- Cut a bird shape from the contrasting fabric scrap

2 With right sides facing, stitch together two pieces of each coordinating fabric in an alternating (A-B-A-B) pattern. Then stitch four lining pieces together with right sides facing.

3 With the seam allowance overlapping, stitch together the batting. Lay the pieced fabric sections, right sides facing, over the batting. Pin the three layers together, and leave one short end open for turning.

4 Stitch ¼ inch (0.6 cm) in from the edge, clip the corners, turn right side out, and press. Turn the open edge in ¼ inch (0.6 cm), press, and pin closed.

5 Carefully topstitch in a straight stitch around the edge of the flat piece once, then again for a sketched look. Complete the quilting by stitching down, then back up, each of the three joined seams.

6 Pin the bird and its wing on one panel. Carefully stitch around the edge of the wing first and then the body at least three times to secure the pieces and add a drawn-on quality to the image. On the bird's head, use a quick back-and-forth motion to stitch an eye and beak. Then add two slightly skewed legs to the bird, stitching back and forth three times. You may prefer to hand embroider the eye, beak, or legs.

7 Bring the two short edges together, and either whip-stitch together by hand or overlap slightly, and topstitch by machine back and forth three times.

woolytote

DESIGNER

ERIN HARRIS

*F*rom the office to a night out, this wooly tote will carry you in style. For added richness, it's lined in silk and features strips of varying patterns and textures.

WHAT YOU NEED

Basic Patchwork Tool Kit (page 11)

¾ yard (68.6 cm) of muslin for foundation

½ yard (45.7 cm) patterned wool for bag top

½ yard (45.7 cm) solid wool for handles

½ yard (45.7 cm) douppioni silk for bag lining, same color as handle wool

Pieces of 10 to 12 different wools in complementary colors for bottom patchwork, 11 inches (27.9 cm) long and varied widths: 3½ to 1½ inches (8.9 to 3.8 cm)

Thread

SEAM ALLOWANCE

Varies

WHAT YOU DO

1. With the rotary cutter, mat, and ruler, cut the following:

- 2 rectangles 8 x 14 inches (20.3 x 35.6 cm) and 2 rectangles 11 x 15 inches (27.9 x 38.1 cm) from the muslin

- 2 rectangles 8 x 14 inches (20.3 x 35.6 cm) from the patterned wool for the top

- 2 rectangles 29½ x 4 inches (74.9 x 10.2 cm) from the solid wool for the handles

- 14 x 28-inch (35.6 x 71.1 cm) rectangle from the silk for the lining

- 15 strips of wool, each 11 inches (27.9 cm) long, in varied widths of 1½ to 3½ inches (3.8 x 8.9 cm)

2. Lay out the two rectangles of muslin on your work surface. They will be used as a foundation for the two lower sides of the bag. Arrange seven or eight of the 15 strips of wool vertically on each of the muslin pieces. Using the foundation-piecing method (see page 21) and a ¼-inch (0.6 cm) seam allowance, piece the two bottom sections of the bag by stitching the strips to the muslin foundation.

3. Press both bottom pieces flat. With your rotary cutter and ruler, square the pieces so they measure 14 x 10 inches (35.6 x 25.4 cm). You may need to restitch the side pieces in place.

4. Pin one of the patterned wool fabric rectangles right side up to each of the foundation pieces, matching edges. Sew in place ¼ inch (0.6 cm) from the left side edge. Press flat, and then sew in place ¼ inch (0.6 cm) from the right side edge. Measure your rectangles, and square to 14 x 8 inches (35.6 x 20.3 cm) if necessary.

5 Pin the top pieces to the bottom pieces, right sides together. Sew together using a ½-inch (1.3 cm) seam allowance. Press seams open.

6 Pin the front of the tote to the back of the tote, matching raw edges. Using a ½-inch (1.3 cm) seam allowance, stitch together along both sides and the bottom of the bag. Clip the bottom corners, and press seams open.

7 Fold the top edge of the bag ½ inch (1.3 cm) toward the inside (wrong side) of the tote and press. Fold another 1½ inches (3.8 cm) toward the inside and press. Turn the tote right side out.

8 To make the lining, match the short sides of the lining rectangle right sides together, and press the fold. This fold is the bottom of your lining. Pin in place along both sides of the lining. Sew the sides together using a ½-inch (1.3 cm) seam allowance.

9 Clip the bottom corners of the lining seam allowance at a 45° angle, and be careful not to clip the stitching. Press the side seams open.

10 Place the lining into the tote, and line up the side seams. Make sure the bottom of the lining is all the way at the bottom of the bag. Slip the top edge of the lining under the folded edge of the bag, and pin in place. Topstitch around the bag 1¼ inches (3.2 cm) from the folded edge.

11 Make the handles by folding short ends of each handle rectangle ½ inch (1.3 cm) toward the wrong side and press. Fold long ends in to meet at the center and press. Fold the strap in half. Press and pin in place. Stitch up both sides of the strap ⅛ inch (0.3 cm) from each side edge.

12 Pin the straps to the bag so the outer side edges are 3 inches (7.6 cm) from the tote's side seams, and the bottom edges are 1 inch (2.5 cm) from the tote's top. Sew in place with a square and an X.

inthebag

$\mathcal{D}$rawn to this bag? It's no wonder. With the adjustable drawstring design, you can carry as little, or as much, as you like. A pretty ribbon cinch-pull with beads tops it off and ties it all together.

DESIGNER

REBEKA LAMBERT

WHAT YOU NEED

Basic Patchwork Tool Kit (page 11)

⅓ yard (30.5 cm) of muslin

½ yard (45.7 cm) fusible interfacing

½ yard (45.7 cm) floral fabric

⅛ yard (11.4 cm) each of 5 different fabrics in complementary colors

Thread

1⅔ yard (152 cm) of ⅜-inch (1 cm) ribbon

Safety pin

2 beads each of 2 different colors

SEAM ALLOWANCE

Varies

WHAT YOU DO

1 Use the rotary cutter, ruler, and cutting mat to cut two 10 x 12-inch (25.4 x 30.5 cm) rectangles from the muslin. Do the same from the interfacing. From the floral fabric, cut a 15½ x 23-inch (26 x 58.4 cm) rectangle.

2 From each of the five printed fabrics, cut out a narrow and a wide wedge piece, using the templates on page 123 as your guide, for a total of ten pieces. Then cut out five narrow wedges and five wide wedges from the interfacing. Fuse the interfacing according to the manufacturer's instructions to the back of the wedges and muslin.

3 From the five printed fabrics, cut out a total of nine 1 x 3-inch (2.5 x 7.6 cm) rectangles and eight 2½ x 3-inch (6.4 x 7.6 cm) rectangles, varying the fabrics.

4 Place two patchwork wedge pieces right sides together. Sew along one long side, using a ¼-inch (0.6 cm) seam allowance (figure 1). Open the pieces with the right sides facing up. Place another wedge face down on top of one of the sewn wedges. Line

up the raw edges, and then stitch using a ¼-inch (0.6 cm) seam allowance. Repeat for all wedges until a bowl is formed.

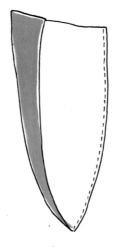

figure 1

5 Sew the fabric rectangles from step 3 together, alternating 1-inch-wide (2.5 cm) and 2½-inch-wide (6.4 cm) rectangles, with a ¼-inch (0.6 cm) seam allowance. You'll have a strip 3 inches (7.6 cm) wide and about 10½ inches (26.7 cm) long. Then cut the patchwork strip in half lengthwise to make two 10½ x 1½-inch (26.7 x 3.8 cm) strips to create a channel for the drawstring.

6 For each strip from step 5, with the wrong side facing up, fold the long sides to the center, then press. Fold each short side over ¼ inch (0.6 cm). Press. Stitch each short end. The finished patchwork channel should be ¾ x 10 inches (1.9 x 25.4 cm). .

7 Pin a patchwork strip, right side up, to the right side of one of the muslin rectangles. The strip should be positioned parallel with the 12-inch (30.5 cm) side, and it should be 3½ inches (8.9 cm) from the top with 1 inch (2.5 cm) of muslin on either end. Then sew the patchwork channel to the muslin, close to the edge, along the long sides of the strip. Repeat with the other piece of muslin and patchwork strip.

8 With the right sides of the muslin together, line up the raw edges and the patchwork channels. Stitch along the sides of the muslin using a ½-inch (1.3 cm) seam allowance.

9 Place the patchwork "bowl" inside the bottom of the muslin body, right sides facing each other. Stitch all around the bowl to join the two together.

10 Make the bag's lining by folding the floral fabric (as cut in step 1) in half, right sides together, lining up the short ends of the rectangle. Stitch along the short end to form a tube. With a needle, thread, and running stitch, gather one end of the tube.

11 Turn the bag body wrong side out and the lining right side out. Place the lining inside the bag body. Sew along the top of the bag ½ inch (1.3 cm) from the edge, and leave a 5-inch (12.7 cm) section unsewn, to be used for turning.

12 Reach through the opening, and pull the lining through the hole, turning the bag right side out. Then press the raw edges of the opening ½ inch (1.3 cm) to the inside, and pin in place. Stitch along the top edge ¼ inch (0.6 cm) from the edge, and be sure to sew up the opening.

13 Cut the ribbon into two equal lengths, and fasten the safety pin onto one end. Starting on one side of the bag, thread a piece of ribbon through both patchwork channels. Repeat, starting on the opposite side of

the bag with the other piece of ribbon. For each side, string beads on the ends of the ribbon, and then tie the two ends together with a knot.

clutchme
tightly

DESIGNER

RENEE PARRILL

*T*his chic clutch is full of personality—and compartments. Featuring a zippered coin purse on the inside, and two additional pockets, this clutch can help you organize your life and look good doing it.

WHAT YOU NEED

Basic Patchwork Tool Kit (page 11)

½ yard (45.7 cm) or scrap of all-cotton quilt batting

½ yard (45.7 cm) of heavyweight interfacing

7 different fabric strips, 2 to 2½ x 20 inches (5.1 to 6.4 x 50.8 cm), cut with rotary cutter and mat

All-purpose thread

1¾ x 32-inch bias strip, cotton

1 yard (91.4 cm) of ⁵⁄₃₂-inch (0.4 cm) cord for piping

Cord foot or zipper foot

¾ yard (68.6 cm) of cotton ticking

9-inch (22.9 cm) zipper

Snap

Snap setter

SEAM ALLOWANCE

½ inch (1.3 cm)

WHAT YOU DO

1 Using the templates on page 124, cut out a piece of cotton batting and a piece of interfacing for both the front and back of the clutch. Place the cotton batting on top of the interfacing for both clutch pieces. Starting from the left edge of the front clutch piece, and leaving enough overhang for seam allowances on all sides, place one strip right side up. Place another strip on top of the first, right sides together, and sew about ¼ inch (0.6 cm) from the cut edge, going through all layers.

2 Repeat this process until the clutch front is pieced, and then do the same for the back piece. Trim both pieces, and make sure to leave a ½-inch (1.3 cm) seam allowance all around. Use the pattern pieces (see the templates on pages 124 and 125) as a guide.

3 For the piping, cut a bias strip 1¾ x 36 inches (4.4 x 91.4 cm). Starting at the bottom center of the clutch back, wrap the bias strip around the cord and sew to the clutch with the cord foot or zipper foot. Make sure to match all cut edges, and clip the bias strip to make going around the curves easy and smooth. Join with a seam at the bottom center, cut the cord to fit, and sew the remaining piping to the clutch.

4 Cut two pieces of cotton ticking for the lining, following the clutch front and back templates on pages 124 and 125. Sew the front lining to the clutch front along the top edge, right sides together.

Open, press, and understitch to keep the lining from rolling to the outside of the clutch. Baste all raw edges together.

5 To make the zippered pocket, cut the ends off the zipper to make it 8 inches (20.3 cm) long. Make fabric stops by folding two small scraps of lining, and stitch one over each zipper end.

6 Following the pocket template on page 125, cut four pieces of the cotton ticking. Take two pieces, right sides together, and center the zipper between them at the top edge. Stitch along the zipper teeth, open, and top-stitch. Repeat on the other side of the zipper, and be sure all pieces remain lined up. Baste the raw edges together, stitching through all four layers.

A FIRM FOUNDATION

The piecing of the front and back of the clutch is an example of foundation piecing, as described on page 21.

7 Place the zippered pocket on the lining side of the clutch front, matching the bottom edges. Baste. Place this piece on the clutch back, right sides together. Sew the pieces together, stitching inside the piping stitching as much as possible. This will hide the stitching on the right side.

8 Place the lining over the clutch so it covers the front, back, and pocket. Sew, leaving open between notches. Turn right side out, and hand stitch closed. Turn again so that the clutch is now completely right-side out. Press.

9 Add the snap at the center front of the clutch flap. Set the male part of the snap into the clutch front so it matches up with the snap on the clutch flap

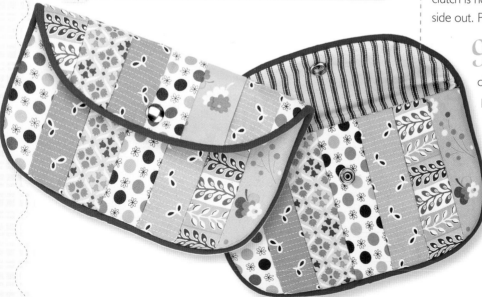

yoga togo

ℋ ere's a way to make your fabric scraps really stretch. With straps long enough to fling over one shoulder and a zippered top to keep your mat securely snug, you'll be practicing the Downright Diva pose in no time.

DESIGNER

VALERIE SHRADER

WHAT YOU NEED

Basic Patchwork Tool Kit (page 11)

Main fabric, ½ yard (45.7 cm)

At least 3 complementary fabrics, ¼ yard (22.9 cm) each

Matching thread

24-inch (61 cm) separating zipper in a complementary color

Zipper foot

¼-inch (0.6 cm) cord for piping, 1 yard (91.4 cm)

SEAM ALLOWANCE

Varies

7 inches (17.8 cm) square. Stack the fabrics, and cut them freehand into about four asymmetrical slices. Create a patchwork rectangle by using one strip from each section. Using a ¼-inch (0.6 cm) seam allowance, stitch the strips together, and press the seams to one side. Make at least three pieced rectangles. Trim each of the rectangles to 5 x 5 inches (12.7 x 12.7 cm). These will be placed in a staggered fashion on the carrier.

4 Cut panels in which to inset the patchwork. Each consists of three pieces, including the patchwork inset. Each finished panel should measure 5 x 16¾ inches (12.7 x 42.5 cm). Cut a strip from each of three different fabrics that is 5 x 13¾ inches (12.7 x 35 cm). Then cut each strip into two pieces with the following measurements:

- First strip: 5 x 2½ inches (12.7 x 6.4 cm) and 5 x 11¼ inches (12.7 x 28.6 cm)

- Second strip: 5 x 3½ inches (12.7 x 8.9 cm) and 5 x 10¼ inches (12.7 x 26 cm)

WHAT YOU DO

1 Cut the following: of the main fabric, two pieces each 8 x 16¾ inches (20.3 x 42.5 cm) and two circular ends 6 inches (15.2 cm) in diameter.

2 On the circular ends, mark the four spots 90° apart that are the "corners" of the circle.

3 Cut six pieces of complementary fabric (you also can include the main fabric used in this project) that are each about

- Third strip: 5 x 4½ inches (12.7 x 11.4 cm) and 5 x 9¼ inches (12.7 x 23.5 cm).

5 Sew one patchwork panel between each piece from each strip, using a ½-inch (1.3 cm) seam. Stitch the panels to one another with a ½-inch (1.3 cm) seam. For added durability, finish the seams, or use a serger to stitch them together.

6 Using the 8 x 16¾-inch (20.3 x 42.5 cm) pieces you cut in step 1, stitch them at either end of the patchwork panel, using a ½-inch (1.3 cm) seam. Trim the piece so it's 16¾ x 26 inches (42.5 x 66 cm).

7 To install the separating zipper, press under ½ inch (1.3 cm) on the long raw edges of the panel. Pin the zipper in place, and center it between the long edges. Separate the zipper, and baste each side in place by hand. Then install the zipper with the zipper foot. Note that you won't stitch a seam at either end of the zipper as with a conventional installation. Be sure to backstitch at the end of each line of stitching.

8 Make bias piping strips about 18 inches (45.7 cm) long for the ends of the carrier. (You'll discard the excess.) Baste each strip in place using a piping or zipper foot. Mark the "corners" of the carrier as you did with the ends in step 2.

9 Turn the carrier inside out, and unzip the zipper partially. With right sides together, pin the circular ends to the body of the carrier, matching the "corner" marks. Clip the carrier body as necessary. Stitch using the piping or zipper foot.

10 For the end flaps that underlie each end of the zipper, choose one of the fabrics, and cut two 2 x 6-inch (5.1 x 15.2 cm) pieces. Cut each piece in half so you have four 2 x 3-inch (5.1 x 7.6 cm) pieces. With right sides together, sew the sets of two pieces to one another, and leave one end free. Turn and press.

11 With the carrier inside out, place a flap at each end of the zipper and center it, with the raw edges even with the raw edges of the carrier. The finished end of the flap faces the opposite end of the zipper. Stitch in place on the existing ½-inch (1.3 cm) seam line.

12 To make the straps, create two patchwork strips, each 3 x 30 inches (7.6 x 76.2 cm). Fold each strip in half lengthwise with right sides facing. Stitch in a ½-inch (1.3 cm) seam, and leave one end free. Turn and trim away the seam on the short end so you can press the strap flat, and place the seam in the middle of the strap. Press under the short raw ends ¼ inch (0.6 cm), and topstitch along both sides.

13 With the carrier right side out, unzip the zipper completely. Pin one strap to the front of the carrier, and place the ends 1½ inches (3.8 cm) below the zipper and directly beside the patchwork inset. Stitch in place, and reinforce with a second line of stitching. Repeat to sew the remaining strip to the front; then stitch both straps in place at a corresponding spot at the back of the carrier.

handy hook holder

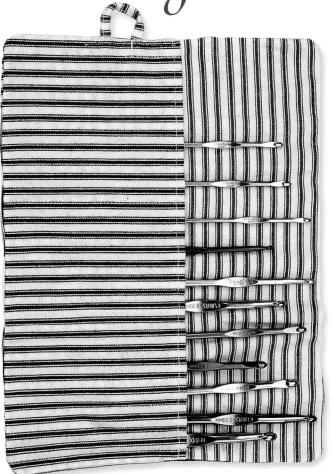

$\mathcal{H}$ooked on crochet? Then this little holder is just for you. Don't know how? Don't dismay—this multi-functional design is also perfect for stashing pens, drawing pencils, manicure sets, makeup brushes and more.

WHAT YOU NEED

Basic Patchwork Tool Kit (page 11)

⅓ yard (30.5 cm) black-striped ticking

⅓ yard (30.5 cm) striped ticking in another color

Thread

2 skeins matching perle cotton or embroidery floss

Self-covering button kit

SEAM ALLOWANCE

⅜ inch (1 cm)

DESIGNER

TERRY TAYLOR

WHAT YOU DO

TO MAKE THE INSIDE:

1 Cut one 12¾ x 9¾-inch (32.4 x 24.7 cm) piece of fabric with the ticking stripes running horizontally.

2 Cut one 12¾ x 5¾-inch (32.4 x 14.6 cm) piece of fabric with the ticking stripes running vertically. Turn and press one long side of the fabric with a ⅜-inch (1 cm) hem.

3 Place the hemmed piece on top of the larger piece. Using the stripes as a guide, stitch along the stripes to create pockets for your hooks. Note that this project calls for seam allowances of ⅜ inch (1 cm).

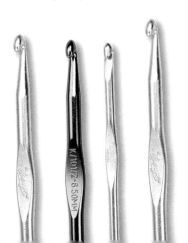

TO MAKE THE OUTSIDE:

4 Cut 12 strips of ticking measuring 2½ x 5½ inches (6.4 x 14 cm) wide. Cut some strips with horizontal stripes, some with vertical stripes.

5 Stack two strips together and stitch along one of the 2½-inch (6.4 cm) ends. Create five more long, two-piece strips in the same way.

6 Arrange the longer strips together as desired. Stitch the long sides together.

7 Embellish the strips with bold running stitches as desired.

TO MAKE THE BUTTON LOOP:

8 Cut a 1 x 4-inch (2.5 x 10.2 cm) strip of fabric. Fold and press the strip in half lengthwise. Open the strip and fold the raw edges in to the crease. Fold the two sides together and stitch the open edges together.

9 Form a U-shaped loop with the fabric. Place the loop on the lower third of the inside fabric, with the loop on top of the fabric. Adjust the size of the loop as desired, and then pin it in place. Trim the ends if needed.

10 Stitch the ends of the loop in place.

ASSEMBLY:

11 Place the inside and outside fabrics right sides together. Pin them in place.

12 To create rounded corners, mark the corners using a coin before you stitch the pieces together.

13 Stitch the two layers together, leaving an opening on the short side with the loop unstitched. You will need the opening in order to turn the assembly right side out.

14 Clip and trim the rounded corners. You may wish to trim the raw edges to reduce bulk.

15 Turn the piece right sides out. Hand stitch the opening closed.

TO MAKE THE BUTTON:

16 Cut a piece of fabric to the size needed for your button.

17 Embellish the fabric with running stitches as desired.

18 Assemble the button according to the manufacturer's instructions.

19 Stitch the button in place about 2½ inches (6.4 cm) in on the side opposite the loop.

TO FINISH:

20 Place your hooks in the pockets, fold the fabric down from the top, fold over the sides, and slip the loop over the button.

tote-ally cute

$\mathcal{T}$his tote is the most. The reverse appliqué method creates a cool peek-a-boo effect when you cut the canvas to reveal the patchwork underneath.

DESIGNER

REBEKA LAMBERT

WHAT YOU NEED

Basic Patchwork Tool Kit (page 11)

½ yard (45.7 cm) canvas in your choice of color

½ yard (45.7 cm) small-print fabric

5 to 7 charm squares in coordinating prints

Thread

Large button and small button in your choice of colors

½ yard (45.7 cm) fleece for interlining

Loop turner

SEAM ALLOWANCE

Varies

WHAT YOU DO

1 From the canvas, use the rotary cutter, cutting mat, and ruler to cut a 15½ x 27-inch (39.4 x 68.6 cm) rectangle for the tote's body. Cut two 2½ x 22-inch (6.4 x 55.9 cm) strips for straps.

2 From the print fabric, cut a 15½ x 27-inch (39.4 x 68.6 cm) rectangle for the lining. Using the patchwork template on page 120, cut 18 pieces from the charm squares.

3 Place two patchwork pieces right sides together. Sew along one long side, using a ¼-inch (0.6 cm) seam allowance. Open the pieces with the right sides facing up. Place another wedge face down on top of one of the sewn wedges. Line up the raw edges, and then stitch using a ¼-inch (0.6 cm) seam allowance. Repeat for all wedges until a circle is formed.

4 On the wrong side of the patchwork circle, press all seams in the same direction. Be sure to press the center to make sure it's flat. It's fine if the center of the circle isn't perfect because it will be covered by a button.

5 Using the flower template on page 120, on the backside of the patchwork circle trace the flower shape using a marker. Be sure to line up the center of the flower template with the center of the circle.

6 Fold the canvas rectangle in half, right sides together, and line up the short ends. Place the marked patchwork circle, face down, about 3½ inches (8.9 cm) from the right edge and 3 inches (7.6 cm) from the top. Pin in place to a single layer of the canvas. Then unfold the canvas, and sew along the flower shape you traced

on the back of the patchwork circle. On the right side of the canvas should be a flower shape made by the stitch lines.

7 With scissors, make a snip in the canvas at the center of the flower. Using the stitch line as your guide, cut away the canvas to reveal the patchwork underneath. Make sure not to cut the patchwork or the stitching. With needle and thread, stitch the buttons to the center of the flower.

8 Fold the canvas in half again, right sides together. The fold is the bottom and the raw edges are the top. Sew along the sides from the top to the fold, using a ½-inch (1.3 cm) seam allowance.

9 Box the bottom corners by centering the side seam along the center of the fold. Mark 2 inches (5.1 cm) across the corner. Stitch. Repeat for the other side.

10 Repeat steps 8 and 9 for both the lining and the fleece. Make the straps by folding a strip of fabric in half lengthwise, right sides together, lining up the long edges. Stitch ¼ inch (0.6 cm)

from the edge. With the loop turner, turn the tube right side out. Press the tube flat. Repeat for the second strap.

11 Turn the bag body wrong side out and the lining right side out. Place the lining inside the bag body; then place the fleece inside the lining. Line up side seams and top edges, and then pin in place.

12 Sandwich the straps between the bag and lining, and pin each strap end 4 inches (10.2 cm) from the outer edge. Starting near a side seam, sew all along the top edge using a ½-inch (1.3 cm) seam allowance, and leave a 5-inch (12.7 cm) section unsewn for turning.

13 Reach through the opening, and pull the lining and fleece interlining through the hole, turning the bag right side out. Press the raw edges of the opening ½ inch (1.3 cm) to the inside, and pin in place. Then stitch along the top edge ¼ inch (0.6 cm) from the edge, and make sure to sew up the opening.

wearable flair

Add these patchwork accessories to make any outfit unforgettable and fun.

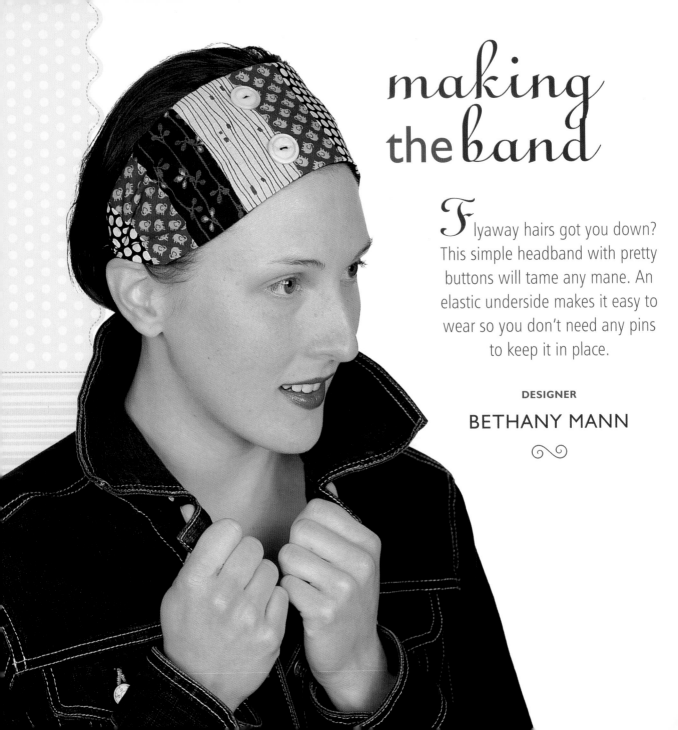

making the band

*F*lyaway hairs got you down? This simple headband with pretty buttons will tame any mane. An elastic underside makes it easy to wear so you don't need any pins to keep it in place.

DESIGNER

BETHANY MANN

WHAT YOU NEED

Basic Patchwork Tool Kit (page 11)

Coordinating cotton prints, maximum size of any one print 4 x 6 inches (10.2 x 15.2 cm)

Thread, 2 colors to coordinate and contrast with fabrics

8 x 15-inch (20.3 x 38.1 cm) solid cotton for backing and elastic casing

Tailor's chalk

8 inches (20.3 cm) of 1-inch-wide (2.5 cm) elastic (preferably non-rolling)

Buttons: 3 small, 2 large

SEAM ALLOWANCE

1/4 inch (0.6 cm)

WHAT YOU DO

1 Cut 10 assorted 2 x 4-inch (5.1 x 10.2 cm) strips with the rotary cutter and ruler. Arrange the pieces in a pattern you choose.

2 Seam each strip end-to-end on the 4-inch (10.2 cm) edge using coordinating thread. Press open all seams.

3 Cut a piece of solid cloth backing 4 x 15 inches (10.2 x 38.1 cm). Sew it along the long sides to the patchwork block with right sides facing. Press all the patchwork seams open.

4 Use the tailor's chalk and ruler to mark diagonal tapers on the last patch at each end. Mark diagonally from the seam to the fabric edge 1 inch (2.5 cm) in from the closest corner. Seam on these marks and trim to a 1/4-inch (0.6 cm) seam allowance. Turn inside out and press.

5 Trim the remaining solid cotton to 12 x 4 inches (30.5 x 10.2 cm), and fold in half lengthwise. Seam the raw edges together down the long side. Turn inside out and press.

6 Topstitch half-channels on each edge with the contrasting thread, and leave a 1 x 8-inch (2.5 x 20.3 cm) channel down the middle. Ruche this center channel casing over the 8-inch (20.3 cm) length of no-roll elastic.

7 Pin ends into the opening on either end of the top part of the headband. Be sure to fold in and pin all raw edges. Try on carefully, and adjust size as necessary. Then double-seam the cased elastic in place to the headband top on each end.

8 To create the pleats where the headband top is seamed to the cased elastic band, fold the patchwork panel in half, and hand stitch a solid tack just beyond the edge of the attached elastic band. Then fold the patchwork panel open, and stitch a solid tack on each edge to keep it in place.

9 Sew the three small buttons on the third patch seam from the right, and sew the two large buttons on the fourth patch seam from the left.

obi*belt*

DESIGNER

BETHANY MANN

*T*ie your outfit all together with an obi belt. Traditionally used to tie a kimono or a martial arts uniform, this one features vintage ties in a knockout design.

WHAT YOU NEED

Basic Patchwork Tool Kit (page 11)

Extra-wide vintage tie

4 x 15-inch (10.2 x 38.1 cm) scraps of 3 assorted fabrics

Coordinating thread

Paper bag or wrapping paper

Wool felt

Solid cotton backing fabric

2 yards (1.8 m) velvet ribbon, ¼ inch (0.6 cm) wide

SEAM ALLOWANCE

½ inch (1.3 cm)

WHAT YOU DO

1 Using your seam ripper, dismantle your vintage tie. Ties are cut in the bias, so cut the front panel from your tie by cutting on a diagonal to keep the grain of the fabric straight for your obi.

2 Determine your waist size. Cut the scraps of assorted fabrics into pieces that are 7 inches by 4 to 6 inches each (17.8 cm x 10.2 to 15.2 cm). Arrange the pieces in a symmetrical pattern to create a piece equal to your waist measurement. If your waist measurement is 28 inches (71.1 cm), for example, the total of the pieces would be 7 x 28 inches (17.8 x 71.1 cm).

3 Seam the patches together on the 7-inch (17.8 cm) edges to create a long, thin rectangle of patchwork. Press open all seams.

4 Cut a piece of paper bag 7 inches (17.8 cm) multiplied by half of your waist measurement. For example, if your waist measurement is 28 inches (71.1 cm), the piece of the paper bag would be 7 x 14 inches (17.8 x 35.6 cm). Fold the paper in half lengthwise, and draw a curved line from the top right corner to about halfway down at the left end. Keep the line as clean and flowing as possible.

MAKING ALLOWANCES

Don't forget about the ½-inch (1.3 cm) seam allowance! If made correctly, the quilted part of the belt should meet neatly in the back with no overlap or gapping.

5 Trim with scissors, and test fit by wrapping the piece around half your waist from belly button to backbone. If you notice gapping or crinkling, trim again, and fold in half to keep it symmetrical. This is your pattern.

6 Use your pattern (wider end on the fold) to trim your patchwork, and cut your wool felt for batting as well as your solid-color cotton backing piece. Trim the felt to ½ inch (1.3 cm) on each end.

7 Layer all the pieces in this order starting at the bottom: patchwork, right side up; solid backing, right side down; felt. Pin together, and then seam down both the long, curved sides.

8 Clip the curves. Then turn inside out and press, turning raw ends to the inside about ½ inch (1.3 cm). Topstitch ¼ inch (0.6 cm) across the top and the bottom of the belt to stabilize it and help it lay flat.

9 Use your machine to stitch around some of the patterns printed on your patches. Work slowly, and don't get too detailed. You can use a contrasting thread in the bobbin to see your handiwork on the backside of the obi.

10 Pin the velvet ribbon in the center of each open end, and topstitch the opening closed as close to the edge as possible, but at least ¼ inch (0.6 cm) from the end to make certain you catch all raw edges.

A FITTING DESIGN

This belt should be designed to lie wide and flat across your belly, curve over your hipbone, and stay straight around to the small of your back. It's made to fit your natural waist.

mintjulephat

T he Kentucky Derby is known as the "most exciting two minutes in sports," but even off the track, you'll look too fabulous in this patchwork hat. From a garden party to a beach vacation, this hat's the winning ticket.

DESIGNER

VALERIE SHRADER

WHAT YOU NEED

Basic Patchwork Tool Kit
(page 11)

Pattern for wide-brimmed hat

Fabric for hat, probably at least
1 yard (91.4 cm), based on pattern

Fabric for patchwork insets, ¼ yard
(22.9 cm) of 5 different prints

Coordinating thread

Notions, such as interfacing and
fusible web, based on pattern

SEAM ALLOWANCE

¼ inch (0.6 cm)

WHAT YOU DO

1 Following the layout from
your pattern, cut out the
fabric for the hat. Set aside.

2 To create the patchwork
insets, begin by cutting six
7 x 9-inch (17.8 x 22.9 cm) pieces
from the fabrics. Include a piece
from the hat fabric.

3 Stack the six pieces of fabric
with the right sides facing up.
Cutting freehand, use the rotary
cutter to slice the stack into six or
seven sections, and make gentle
curves as desired (figure 1).

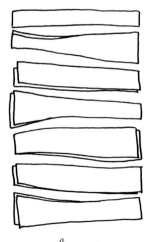

figure 1

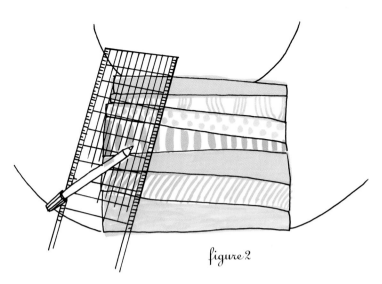

figure 2

4 Create a patchwork rectangle by using one strip from each section. Using a ¼-inch (0.6 cm) seam allowance, stitch the strips together, and press the seams to one side. Make about four pieced rectangles, depending on your hat pattern.

5 To insert the patchwork, you'll cut a corresponding piece or pieces from the brim, and stitch the patchwork inset in its place. To begin, place one rectangle on the fabric piece you cut for the brim.

6 With the brim pattern piece as a guide, mark and then trim the patchwork rectangle to fit the curves of the brim (figure 2).

Remember to include a ¼-inch (0.6 cm) seam allowance on each side. Trim as many rectangles as desired.

7 Place a trimmed patchwork piece on the fabric piece you cut for the brim, and mark its desired location. Don't forget to factor in the side-seam allowances you'll use to stitch the patchwork inset to the brim piece. Before

you cut, be sure to include an extra ¼ inch (0.6 cm) on both pieces.

8 Trim the shape of the inset away from the brim where marked. With right sides together, stitch the patchwork inset into the brim piece, using a ¼-inch (0.6 cm) seam allowance. Grade the seam, and closely trim the inset. Check the accuracy of your inset by comparing the brim to the paper pattern piece if necessary.

9 Repeat steps 6 through 8 to insert the patchwork into the crown of the hat and along the brim as desired.

10 Follow the instructions in your pattern to construct the hat. If the pattern calls for a bias binding, as in this project, include strips from the patchwork fabrics as well.

MAKING IT ACROSS

You may need to stitch two of the rectangles together to span the brim. If so, use a ¼-inch (0.6 cm) seam. In this project, the patchwork rectangles were trimmed so they were wide at the bottom.

belt it out

$\mathcal{D}$o you want to get the belt? Well, then stop what you're doing and make one! With groovy cotton prints and an adjustable loop, you'll be amazed how fun these are to make—and wear.

DESIGNER

ERIN HARRIS

WHAT YOU NEED

Basic Patchwork Tool Kit (page 11)

Small amounts of 8 to 12 different cotton prints, each at least 2 x 4 inches (5.1 x 10.2 cm)

Thread

1/4 yard (22.9 cm) of 45-inch (1.14 m) wide heavy fusible interfacing

2 D-rings, each 1 1/2 inches (3.8 cm)

SEAM ALLOWANCE

Varies

WHAT YOU DO

1 Take your belt measurement around your waist or hips, and add 6 inches (15.2 cm) to the number to get what we'll call measurement Y. That gives you about a 5-inch (12.7 cm) overlap when you pass the belt through the D-rings.

2 With the rotary cutter and ruler, cut your fabric into 4-inch (10.2 cm) strips of various widths with no piece narrower than 2 inches (5.1 cm).

3 Lay out your fabric as you choose. Starting from the left, sew your strips right sides together along the 4-inch (10.2 cm) side

using a 1/4-inch (0.6 cm) seam allowance. (See page 20 for more on this strip-piecing technique.) Keep piecing left to right until your strip is equal in length to your measurement Y. Press all seams open.

4 Cut a piece of the interfacing into a strip that is 3 inches high and 1 inch shorter than your meaurement Y from step 1. With the wrong side of the belt facing up, center the interfacing on the belt, fusible side down, and leave a 1/2-inch (1.3 cm) border on all sides.

5 Iron the interfacing onto your belt following the manufacturer's instructions. Fold in both short ends of the belt 1/2 inch

(1.3 cm), and press in place. Fold the top and bottom of the belt down 1/2 inch (1.3 cm), and press in place.

6 Fold the belt in half and press. Pin in place. Starting at one end, sew your belt together by topstitching 1/8 inch (0.3 cm) from the open edge. At the corners, keep your needle in the down position, and pivot 90°. Continue until you have topstitched all four sides of the belt.

7 insert an inch (2.5 cm) of the belt through the D-rings, and fold it over. Topstitch two parallel lines about 1/4 inch (0.6 cm) apart to secure the D-rings. Backstitch at both ends of both lines to make sure the belt won't come apart.

flowing scarf

This silk scarf is not about perfection; it's about improvisation. The fabrics used are notoriously tricky to sew, so don't fret over irregular seams. Let the fabrics do their thing, and just go with the flow.

DESIGNER

VALERIE SHRADER

WHAT YOU NEED

Basic Patchwork Tool Kit (page 11)

Scraps of lightweight fabrics, such as silk chiffon, china silk, kimono remnants, and cotton batiste

Thread, neutral color

Decorative, variegated rayon thread, two complementary colors

SEAM ALLOWANCE

1/2 inch (1.3 cm)

WHAT YOU DO

1 Cut a series of strips from the scraps in varying widths, but none less than 2 inches (5.1 cm) wide. Construct seven 9 x 9-inch (22.9 x 22.9 cm) patchwork blocks by stitching them with the wrong sides together using the neutral thread. Trim each block to 8 1/2 x 8 1/2 inches (19 x 19 cm).

2 Embellish and finish the blocks by stitching the seam allowances down with one color of the rayon thread. Use a double strand to intensify the sheen and play with the color gradations. Vary your stitches if desired.

3 Stitch the blocks to one another using a 1/2-inch (1.3 cm) seam with either the right or wrong sides facing, as desired. Embellish the seam allowances as you did in step 2 with the second color of rayon thread.

4 Press under a narrow double hem along each of the long edges, pressing each hem to a different side of the scarf. Use a running stitch to secure the hem, sewing by hand and using the rayon thread of your choice. Repeat to hem the remaining short edges.

too cool cuff

A cuff this cool is twice as nice with reversible snaps that let you show off your best side. Any way you flip it, this cuff's the stuff.

DESIGNER

LAUREN HUNT

WHAT YOU NEED

Basic Patchwork Tool Kit (page 11)

⅛ yard (11.4 cm) muslin

Strips of coordinating cotton fabrics, 1 to 4 inches (2.5 to 10.2 cm) wide and at least 4½ inches (11.4 cm) long.

2 strips of coordinating cotton fabrics, 1 to 2 inches (2.5 to 5 cm) wide and 9 to 11 inches (22.9 to 27.9 cm) long.

Coordinating rickrack in one or two colors

Cotton quilting thread, in white and in the colors of your rickrack

Double-sided fusible webbing

Decorative snaps and snap attachment device

SEAM ALLOWANCE

¼ inch (0.6 cm)

WHAT YOU DO

1 With a measuring tape, determine the measurement around your wrist at the desired tightness for the cuff. Add 1½ inches (3.8 cm) to this length to get the length of muslin you will need. For example, my wrist measurement is 8 inches (20.3 cm), so my muslin length is 9½ inches (24.1 cm).

2 Cut your muslin to the length you have determined, and then cut one piece from it 4½ inches (11.4 cm) wide and another 3 inches (7.6 cm) wide.

3 Place your 4½-inch (11.4 cm) muslin piece horizontally on your work surface. Lay out your cotton strips on it vertically in the order you wish to piece them in. Remembering that the strips will be sewn with a ¼ inch (0.6 cm) seam allowance, lay them out taking account of that loss of width. Lay out two or three pieces of rickrack between the strips as well.

4 When you have the strips and rickrack where you want them, trim them to the width of the muslin. Now you will begin the piecing. Move your strips of cotton off of your muslin, but keep them in the order you ave determined.

5 Start with the first strip on the left-hand side, and pin it, face up, to the left side of the muslin. Sew the right edge of that strip to the muslin ¼ inch (0.6 cm) from the strip's edge. Now take your second strip and pin it, top sides facing, directly on top of the first strip with their right edges aligned. Turn the muslin over, and sew a line to the left of your first, attaching the second strip to both the first and the muslin. Turn back over and press flat.

6 Continue to piece in this fashion, but sewing the strips together ¼ inch (0.6 cm) from the edge from the top instead of the bottom as you just did, until you have reached the end of your muslin.

ing strips on either side of the pre-pieced strip cut from your first pieced muslin. (See the photo, near left.)

10 When the second muslin is pieced, trim it like the first and then pin the two muslins together, top sides facing. Sew along the left, top, and right sides; backstitch at the beginning and end and at both corners, but leave the bottom edge open. Cut the top left and right corners to make it easier to turn out.

11 Turn inside out, pushing corners out, then press. Fold the bottom edge of both sides inward, pressing as you go. Make sure the sides align evenly. Cut a piece of double-sided fusible webbing 2 inches (5 cm) wide and ½ inch (1.3 cm) shorter than your cuff length.

12 Peel one side of the paper off. Stick the webbing, sticky side down, into the cuff, aligning the edge with the edge

7 Sew on the rickrack pieces through their centers, matching your thread to your rickrack so it will blend in. Turn your pieced muslin over and trim any overhanging strips, using the muslin and a ruler as your guide.

8 Measure 1½ inches (3.8 cm) down on your muslin width, and cut across the entire piece

horizontally. This will leave you with two pieces of muslin, one 3 inches (7.6 cm) wide and one 1½ inches (3.8 cm) wide.

9 Take the 3-inch-wide (7.6 cm) muslin piece, and piece it using the same general technique as you did above. This time, run the strips horizontally, using the two longer coordinat-

of the ironed edge. Make sure the webbing is stuck down and unwrinkled, then peel the top layer of paper off. With your hands, press the cuff together, checking that the bottom ironed edges meet, and then iron according to the instructions for the fusible webbing.

13 Attach snaps to the right and left edges, using decorative snap covers on the back of both the male and female snaps.

PUTTING IT TOGETHER

The strips in this project are assembled using the foundation-piecing method, described on page 21 of the Basics section.

95

beautiful accents

These patchwork pieces will add a stylish
touch to any room in your home.

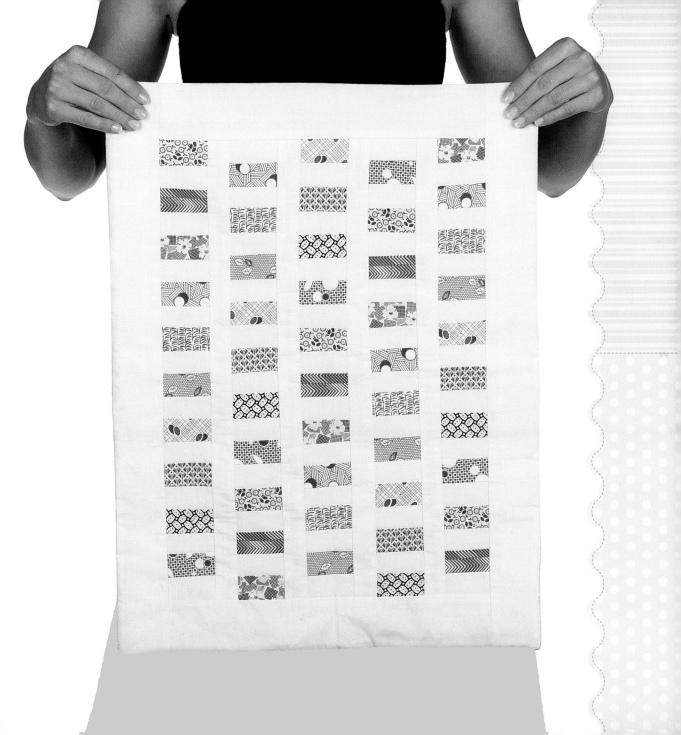

sublimetime

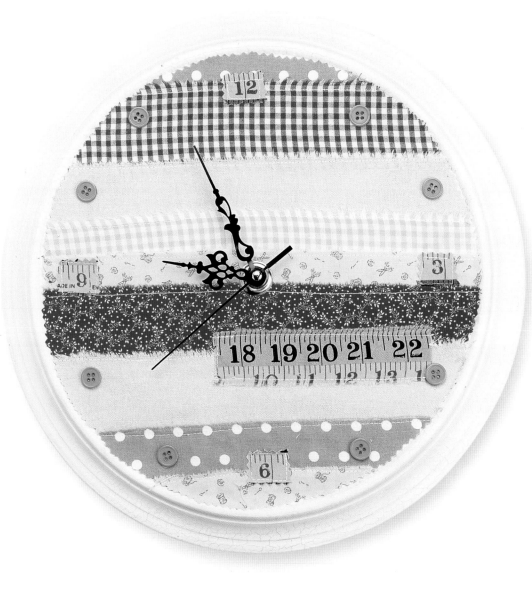

*T*ime flies when you're having fun making this patchwork clock. With hand-torn strips of fabric, and buttons to mark the hour, this is one clock you'll want to watch.

WHAT YOU NEED

Basic Patchwork Tool Kit (page 11)

Scraps (less than ⅛ yard [11.4 cm]) of six different fabrics in two complementary shades along with natural linen

Round, wooden clock with a flat face

¼ yard (22.9 cm) of lightweight cotton fabric

Thread in same color as cotton fabric

Pinking shears

Fabric glue or white glue

Grommet

8 to 12 small, flat buttons

SEAM ALLOWANCE

¼ inch (0.6 cm)

DESIGNER

AUTUM HALL

WHAT YOU DO

1 Tear your fabric in random-size strips 1 to 2½ inches (2.5 to 6.4 cm) wider and 1 inch (2.5 cm) longer than the diameter of your clock face. The 12-inch-diameter (30.5 cm) clock pictured here required 12 strips.

2 Sew the strips onto your cotton fabric, and overlap until you have enough to cover the size of your clock.

3 Trace a circle the size of your clock onto the fabric, and cut it out with the pinking shears. Find the circle's center, and make a small hole for inserting the grommet.

4 Remove the hands from the clock. Apply the fabric glue liberally to the clock, and place the fabric on the clock face with a grommet over the center post.

5 Replace the hands. Glue the buttons in place where clock numbers would be. Leave the piece flat to dry completely before hanging.

HANDY HARDWARE

"Grommets" may sound like something you'd find in a book involving Harry Potter. Actually, these helpful metal, plastic, or rubber rings can be found at your local hardware or craft store.

sew pretty
ornaments

Make these exquisite little ornaments for friends and family, or stitch up a bunch for your own seasonal decor. Unlike glass ornaments, these hand-sewn beauties won't break, so you can enjoy them year after year.

DESIGNER

JOAN K. MORRIS

WHAT YOU NEED

Basic Patchwork Tool Kit (page 11)

Scrap paper

6 assorted similar fabrics

Matching thread

8 x 8-inch (20.3 x 20.3 cm) piece of felt

8 inches (20.3 cm) of gold cord

Knitting needle

15 inches (38.1 cm) matching trim or ribbon

Hot glue gun

SEAM ALLOWANCE

¼ inch (0.6 cm)

WHAT YOU DO

1 Draw out your ornament design on the scrap paper, and cut it out. Draw a rectangle 1¼ x 4 inches (3.2 x 10.2 cm), and cut it out.

2 Using the rectangle pattern, cut out three rectangles from each of the six fabrics. Choose two fabrics, and cut two 2 x 4-inch (5.1 x 10.2 cm) rectangles from each.

3 Lay out the fabrics in the pattern of the ornaments: six small rectangles vertically, two small rectangles horizontally under that, a large rectangle on top, and a large one at the bottom (figure 1). You will have two sets.

figure 1

4 Machine stitch the vertical pieces together with a ¼-inch (0.6 cm) seam allowance. Press the seams open. Machine stitch the horizontal pieces to the bottom. Press seam open. Stitch one of the large rectangles to the bottom and one to the top, and center them on the piece. Repeat this for the second set.

5 Place the felt on the wrong side of one of the pieces. Place its matching piece right sides together with the first. Trim a little of the felt off. Cut a 6-inch (15.2 cm) piece of the gold cord, and fold it in half. Place the cord between the two pieces, with the cut end up.

6 Place the ornament pattern in position on top of the piece, and pin in place. Machine stitch around the outside of the pattern. Leave open a small section at the bottom to allow turning right side out. Clip curves, and turn right side out. Push out corners with the knitting needle. Press flat, folding the opening inside. Hand stitch the opening closed. Use the hot glue gun to hold the trim in place.

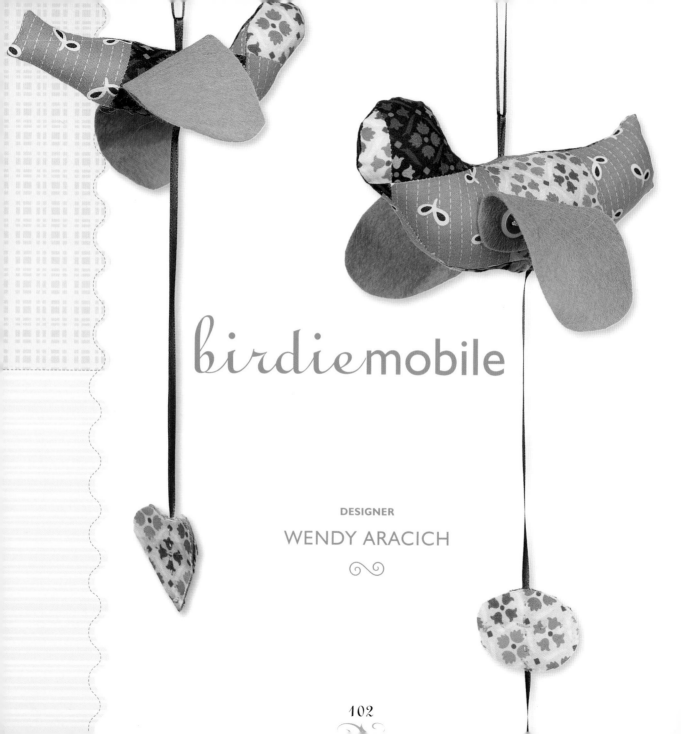

birdiemobile

DESIGNER

WENDY ARACICH

This adorable patchwork mobile is a bright, cheery addition to any room. Felt wings are attached with a button for added movement, and the lightweight balsa support makes it easy to display.

WHAT YOU NEED

Basic Patchwork Tool Kit (page 11)

1/4 yard (22.9 cm) or 1 fat quarter each of three fabrics

5 yards (4.5 m) of 1/8-inch-wide (0.3 cm) ribbon

Thread

Wing template

6 assorted buttons, each 5/8 inch (1.6 cm)

Embroidery needle

Embroidery floss

Cotton or polyester stuffing

Remnant wool felt

Piece of balsa wood, 1/2 inch (1.3 cm) square and 18 inches (45.7 cm) long

SEAM ALLOWANCE

1/4 inch (0.6 cm)

WHAT YOU DO

1 Cut 16 squares, each 2½ inches (6.4 cm), from all three fabrics. In a somewhat random pattern, arrange the squares on a work surface in a rectangle of seven columns and six rows.

2 Beginning with the first row, pin the right edge of the first square to the left edge of the second square with right sides together. Next, pin the right edge of the second square to the left edge of the third square. Continue pinning in this fashion until all squares in the top row are pinned. Set aside and repeat with remaining rows.

3 Machine stitch along pinned edges with a ¼-inch (0.6 cm) seam allowance. Press seams open. Join rows from top to bottom along common edges, taking care to match the vertical seams. Press seams open.

4 On wrong side of the fabric, trace the large bird template four times and the small bird template two times. (See the templates on page 121). Cut the birds carefully along the traced line. Set scraps aside.

5 Cut three 2-inch (5.1 cm) pieces of ribbon. Fold one piece in half. Align the bottom edges of the ribbon with the top edge of one piece of the large bird (right side up), and pin in place. Place the corresponding bird piece on top, right sides together, and pin around edges, leaving the bottom open where indicated. Repeat with the two remaining birds.

6 Machine stitch around each bird with a ½-inch (1.3 cm) seam allowance, and leave the bottom open where indicated on the template. Trim seams, and turn right side out.

7 Pin the wings to the birds where indicated on the template. Place a button over the wing. With the embroidery needle and embroidery floss, sew the button to the wing, and make sure to go through both the wing and the top layer of the bird, but not the bottom layer of the bird. Repeat until all wings are attached.

8 Stuff the birds with stuffing. Tuck under seams of openings on each bird and pin. Close the opening by hand with a small running stitch.

9 Fold a saved scrap in half, right sides together, and pin to hold. With a pencil or dressmaker's chalk, draw a heart shape freehand on the fabric. Lay the cut heart on a piece of felt, and cut out one heart from the felt. Layer the felt heart between patchwork hearts, right sides out, and pin to hold. In the same fashion as the heart, make and cut two ovals and two leaves. Pin together with felt in the center.

10 Cut an 8-inch (20.3 cm) piece of ribbon, and sandwich it between the top and middle layers of the heart so the bottom of the ribbon is inside the heart, and the remainder extends out from the top of the heart. Embroider a running stitch from top to bottom through the center of the heart, taking care to catch the ribbon with the stitches. Next, embroider a running stitch from left to right through the center of the heart, taking care to catch the ribbon with the stitches.

11 Cut two 13-inch (33 cm) pieces of ribbon. Sandwich one ribbon between an oval, with about the same amount of ribbon extending out from the top and bottom of the oval. Stitch two rows of embroidery, one top to bottom and one left to right, taking care to catch the ribbon with your stitches. Repeat for the other oval.

OUT OF HARM'S WAY

For safety reasons, don't hang your mobile—with its enticing buttons—over a crib or other spot where it will be within reach of the busy hands (and mouths) of babies or toddlers.

12 Sandwich the end of the ribbon coming from an oval between a leaf, with the bottom of the ribbon inside the leaf. Attach the leaf to the ribbon as you did the ovals in step 11. Repeat for the other leaf.

13 Cut one 30-inch (75 cm) and two 26-inch (66 cm) pieces of ribbon. Thread one of the 26-inch pieces through the loop on one of the larger birds. Tie it to the wood support about two inches from the left end. Bring the ribbon around the support, and tie in a simple knot, leaving at least a 4-inch (10.2 cm) tail. Loop the ends down around the support, and tie a second knot beneath the support. Finally, bring the loops back around the top of the support, and tie in a bow. Trim excess ribbon if needed. Repeat with the remaining birds, tying the smaller bird in the center of the support and the other large bird around two inches from the right end.

14 Cut a 50-inch (1.25 m) piece of ribbon. Thread the ribbon from left to right under the ties on the wood support. Pull through to bring the ends together, and form a triangle. Tie the ends together with a knot and bow, and adjust to the desired length for hanging.

NO LUMBERJACK REQUIRED

You can find balsa wood in various sizes at your local craft store. A ½-inch-square (1.3 cm) piece will be thin and light enough that you can easily cut it to the required length with a utility knife.

sitting pretty cushion

Move over, curds and whey—this little cushion turns Miss Muffet into Miss Magnifique. With sweet ribbon detailing, rickrack, and beads, you'll be sitting pretty in no time.

DESIGNER

JOAN K. MORRIS

WHAT YOU NEED

Basic Patchwork Tool Kit (page 11)

15-inch-round (38.1 cm) pillow form with flat sides

6 assorted print cotton fabrics, ¼ yard (21.6 cm) each

Paper-backed fusible web

6 assorted ribbons, rickrack, and trim

Invisible thread

Matching thread

10 to 12 glass beads or buttons

½ yard (45.7 cm) striped upholstery fabric

3 yards (2.7 m) of cord for piping

½ yard (45.7 cm) more of one of the print cotton fabrics for the piping

Zipper foot

Spray adhesive

1 yard (.91 cm) quilt batting

1 yard (.91 m) light colored embroidery floss

Embroidery needle (long with large eye)

2 covered buttons, 1¼ inch (3.2 cm)

SEAM ALLOWANCE

½ inch (1.3 cm)

WHAT YOU DO

1 Trace the pillow form onto the scrap paper. Add ½ inch (1.3 cm) all the way around the edge, and cut out. Fold the circle in half, and then fold the half in thirds to get the size of the six triangles minus the seam allowance. Trace the shape, and add ½ inch (1.3 cm) to the sides. Cut this out.

2 With this pattern, cut out a triangle from each of the six print cotton fabrics. Machine stitch three triangles side by side with a ½-inch (1.3 cm) seam allowance. Pin the seams before sewing if needed. Press the seams flat, then machine stitch the other three triangles together, and press flat. Pin the two pieces together, and machine stitch to create the circle. Press the seam open.

3 Cut out 6-inch (15.2 cm) squares of each of the six fabrics, and cut six 6-inch (15.2 cm) squares of the fusible web. Following the manufacturer's instructions, adhere it to the back of each of the pieces of fabric. On the paper backing, draw the flowers, circles, and leaves you want to place on the pillow. Cut the flowers out.

4 Position the flowers on the cushion top, and add the ribbons as stems until you get a design you like. Remove the flowers, leaving the ribbon in place, and pin in position. With invisible thread in the top of the machine and matching thread in the bobbin, machine zigzag the ribbon in place.

5 Following the manufacturer's instructions, remove the paper backing, and iron the flowers and leaves in position. On top of the flowers, iron on the centers.

Machine zigzag the flowers and leaves in position with the invisible thread on top and regular thread in the bobbin. Place the 10 to 12 glass beads and buttons in position, and hand stitch them with needle and thread.

6 From the striped fabric, cut a circle the same size as the

top cushion. Cut out a strip 3 inches (7.6 cm) wide from the striped fabric with a length that equals the total measurement around the pillow plus 1/2 inch (1.3 cm).

7 Measure around the pillow, and add 2 inches (5.1 cm) to the measurement. This will be the length of each of the two pieces of piping. Cut the fabric on the diagonal, and make it 2 inches wide by the length measured. You'll need to piece fabric together to make it long enough. When piecing bias, place the ends of the fabric at 90° angles, stitch from corner to corner, and cut off the excess corner.

8 To make the piping, place the cord in the center of the fabric you cut in step 7 and, with the zipper foot, stitch as close as you can to the cord.

9 With the zipper foot still on, machine baste the piping in place on the top and bottom pieces. Do this by placing the piping around the edge, with the raw edge of the piping lining up with the raw edge of the circle. Start stitching 1 inch (2.5 cm) from the edge of the piping. Where the two ends meet, cut the piping cord to

the exact length. Put the two ends right sides together, and stitch across at the proper length. Push the cord back in place, and finish stitching the piping.

10 Cut pieces of the quilt batting to cover the pillow form, and glue in place with the spray adhesive. Place the cushion top upside down on the pillow form. Wrap the 3-inch (7.6 cm) strip of striped fabric around the form, wrong side out. Pin the edges of the top and the side strip together and stitch in a 1/2-inch (1.3 cm) seam allowance, using a zipper foot. Stitch the ends of the 3-inch (7.6 cm) strip together.

11 Stitch the bottom piece to the other side of the 3-inch (7.6 cm) strip; leave open about a third so the pillow will fit inside. Clip curves. Turn right side out.

12 Stuff the pillow inside. Pin the opening closed, and then hand stitch the opening closed.

13 Thread the embroidery floss onto the needle, and double the thread. From the top, run the needle through the center of the pillow to the back, leaving half the embroidery floss on top. Run the needle back up to the front. Pull both ends of the embroidery floss tight, tie a knot, and pull it tightly.

14 Following the manufacturer's instructions, cover the two buttons with the striped fabric. With regular thread and needle, stitch one of the covered buttons on each side.

PIECE IT TOGETHER

If you don't have a piece of fabric that can make a strip in the length you need in step 6, piece one together. If you do, add a 1/2-inch (1.3 cm) seam allowance between the pieces.

mini mod
coin quilt

$\mathcal{M}$ake a mini art quilt like this one to hang on your wall, dress up an armchair, or use as a chic table runner. The piecework is surprisingly easy to do and perfect for the first-time quilter.

DESIGNER

MAITREYA DUNHAM

WHAT YOU NEED

Basic Patchwork Tool Kit (page 11)

1 1/2 x 13-inch (3.8 x 33 cm) strips of 10 patterned fabrics

10 strips of coordinating solid fabric such as unbleached muslin, each 1 1/2 x 13 inches (3.8 x 33 cm)

Thread in a coordinating color

4 strips of solid fabric, each 1 1/2 x 21 inches (3.8 x 53.3 cm)

2 strips of solid fabric, each 3 x 15 inches (7.6 x 38.1 cm)

2 strips of solid fabric, each 3 x 25 inches (7.6 x 63.5 cm)

25 x 20-inch (63.5 x 50.8 cm) piece of thin batting

25 x 20-inch (63.5 x 50.8 cm) piece of backing fabric

1 skein embroidery floss in a coordinating color

SEAM ALLOWANCE

1/4 inch (0.6 cm)

WHAT YOU DO

1 With your rotary cutter, cut all fabric pieces as indicated at left.

2 Sew together all 20 of the 13-inch (33 cm) pieces in strips along long edges, right sides together, alternating a patterned fabric with the solid fabric. Press the seams toward the patterned fabric strips.

3 Sew the last strip to the first strip to create a loop, then trim uneven ends. Slice the piece into five loops 2½ inches (6.4 cm) wide. With your seam ripper, open a different seam of each loop. You will have five 2½-inch (6.4 cm) wide strips, each with alternating patterned and solid fabrics. Press the strips again.

4 Arrange as you wish, alternating the orientation of strips so every other strip is offset. For example, the first, third, and fifth strips could have pattern blocks on top, and the second and fourth strips solid blocks on top.

5 Sew each patchwork strip to a 21-inch (53.3 cm) solid strip, right sides together. Trim the excess and press.

6 Sew the 3 x 15-inch (7.6 x 38.1 cm) strips to the narrow ends of the patchwork section. Trim the excess and press. Then sew the 3 x 25-inch (7.6 x 63.5 cm) strips to long sides. Press. Square up all sides and corners by trimming to about a 2½-inch (6.4 cm) border of solid material all around.

7 Cut the backing fabric and batting 1 inch (2.5 cm) larger all around than the quilt top. Layer the batting, backing fabric (right side up), and quilt top (right side down). Pin through all layers.

8 Stitch around the edge of the quilt top, leaving a gap to turn. Trim the excess fabric and batting. Clip corners.

9 Turn the quilt through the gap, and pay attention to making nice corners. Press edges flat, and stitch the gap shut.

10 Thread a needle with about 18 inches (45.7 cm) of three strands of embroidery floss. In the center of each patterned rectangle, sew through all layers, from the back to the top, then back down again ⅛ inch (0.3 cm) away from the first hole. Go directly to the next patterned rectangle in the row without cutting the thread, and repeat this up-and-down sewing in each patterned rectangle around the quilt.

11 Flip the quilt to the back, and cut in the middle of each stretch of floss. Tie the ends of the floss coming from one rectangle in a knot, and trim the ends. Repeat over the rest of the quilt.

MAKING CHANGE

Quilts with stacked rectangles, also known as Chinese coin quilts, are said to be inspired by the shapes of coins once used in China.

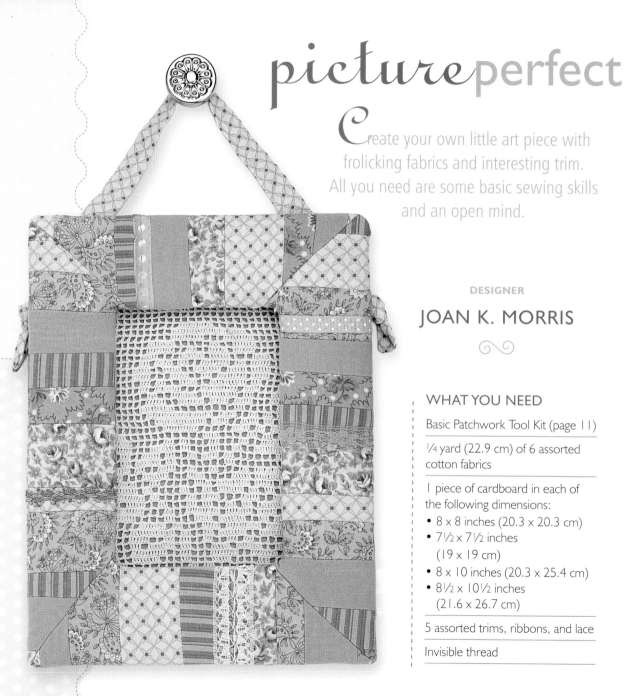

pictureperfect

Create your own little art piece with frolicking fabrics and interesting trim. All you need are some basic sewing skills and an open mind.

DESIGNER

JOAN K. MORRIS

WHAT YOU NEED

Basic Patchwork Tool Kit (page 11)

1/4 yard (22.9 cm) of 6 assorted cotton fabrics

1 piece of cardboard in each of the following dimensions:
- 8 x 8 inches (20.3 x 20.3 cm)
- 7 1/2 x 7 1/2 inches (19 x 19 cm)
- 8 x 10 inches (20.3 x 25.4 cm)
- 8 1/2 x 10 1/2 inches (21.6 x 26.7 cm)

5 assorted trims, ribbons, and lace

Invisible thread

Matching thread

Craft knife

Spray adhesive

2 pieces quilt batting, 10 x 10 inches (25.4 x 25.4 cm) and 10 x 12 inches (25.4 x 30.5 cm)

½ yard (45.7 cm) fabric in your choice of color

5 x 5-inch (12.7 x 12.7 cm) scrap of lace

6 x 8-inch (15.2 x 20.3 cm) scrap of lace

Hot glue gun

SEAM ALLOWANCE

¼ inch (0.6 cm)

WHAT YOU DO

1 With the rotary cutter, cut strips of the assorted cotton fabric 1 to 2 inches (2.5 to 5.1 cm) wide. For the 8 x 8-inch (20.3 x 20.3 cm) frame, the strips should be 11 inches (27.9 cm) long. Cut enough so that, when sewn together, it will be 11 inches (27.9 cm) wide. For the 8 x 10-inch (20.3 x 25.4 cm) frame, the strips should be 8 inches (20.3 cm) long. Cut enough so that, when sewn, they will be 22 inches (55.9 cm) wide.

2 For the 8 x 8-inch (20.3 x 20.3 cm) frame, lay out the pieces in order, and machine stitch them side by side. Press the seams open.

3 For the 8 x 10-inch (20.3 x 25.4 cm) frame, line up the pieces in order, and machine stitch them side by side. Press the seams open. Cut the sewn piece in half lengthwise, so you have two pieces 4 x 22 inches (10.2 x 55.9 cm). Cut a 10-inch (25.4 cm) and 12-inch (30.5 cm) piece from each strip.

4 Place ribbon, lace, and trim in position on the 8 x 8-inch (20.3 x 20.3 cm) frame piece and the 8 x 10-inch (20.3 x 25.4 cm) frame piece. Machine sew them with invisible thread in the top and regular thread in the bobbin. You can zigzag or run straight stitches down the sides.

5 For the 8 x 8-inch (20.3 x 20.3 cm) frame, cut a center hole 3 x 3 inches (7.6 x 7.6 cm) in the 8 x 8-inch (20.3 x 20.3 cm) cardboard with the craft knife and ruler. For the

8 x 10-inch (20.3 x 25.4 cm) piece, cut a 4 x 6-inch (10.2 x 15.2 cm) hole in the center. With the spray adhesive, glue down the quilt batting to the front of the cutout cardboard frames, and wrap it to the back. Cut an X in the center, and fold the batting to the back.

6 For the backs of each frame, take the 7 1/2 x 7 1/2-inch (19 x 19 cm) piece of cardboard and the 8 1/2 x 10 1/2-inch (19 x 21 cm) piece of cardboard, and using the spray adhesive, adhere the 1/2 yard (45.7 cm) of fabric of your choice to both sides. The fabric from the back side should wrap around to the front. The front needs to cover 1 inch (2.5 cm) beyond the opening. Center the lace scraps on the front of the back pieces, and use the spray adhesive to hold them.

7 Cut two strips of one of your fabrics that are each 2 1/2 x 20 inches (6.4 x 50.8 cm). Fold them in half lengthwise, machine stitch 1/2 inch (1.3 cm) in from the edge, and stitch one end of each piece.

Turn right side out with a pencil. Press flat, and fold the open end closed. Machine stitch across this. Tie knots in all four ends, leaving 1/2 inch (1.3 cm) to the ends.

8 For the 8 x 10-inch (20.3 x 25.4 cm) frame, take the cut pieces you cut in step 3, and lay the long ones on the 10-inch (25.4 cm) side and the shorter ones on the 8-inch (20.3 cm) side with the wrong sides up. Miter the corners by making a seam that runs from the outside corner to the inside corner. Pin in place, and machine stitch on the pin line. Cut off the excess fabric. Press the seams open.

9 To cover the 8 x 8-inch (20.3 x 20.3 cm) frame, place the batting-covered cardboard in the center of the sewn

piece. Turn the corners in, and glue in place with hot glue. Work your way around the outside edge, using the hot glue as you go. Cut an X in the center with the craft knife, fold the pieces to the back, and glue. Repeat for the 8 x 10-inch (20.3 x 25.4 cm) piece.

10 Use hot glue to adhere the ties in place on the top of the back pieces. Place hot glue around the sides and bottom edges of the back piece. Leave the top open in case you want to slide a photo into the frame. Quickly center the front piece over the back and press.

IT WAS HERE A MINUTE AGO

Invisible thread is not truly invisible—if it was, how could you ever find it at the fabric store? But this clear, very fine nylon thread is a good choice when you want the fabric, not the stitches, to be the star of your piece.

pillowtalk

Create the patchwork pillow of your dreams with squares of your favorite fabrics. For easy cleaning, this pillow is designed with a zipper so you can remove the cover as needed.

WHAT YOU NEED

Basic Patchwork Tool Kit (page 11)

⅓ yard (30.5 cm) each of two main colors in various fabrics

Thread

14-inch (35.6 cm) all-purpose zipper, same color as thread

Masking tape

Zipper foot

18-inch (45.7 cm) square pillow insert

SEAM ALLOWANCE

¼ inch (0.6 cm)

DESIGNER

WENDI GRATZ

WHAT YOU DO

1 Cut 25 squares 4 x 4 inches (10.2 x 10.2 cm) each of your first color. Then cut 25 squares 4 x 4 inches (10.2 x 10.2 cm) of your second color.

2 Lay out one side of the pillow. Start with a square of the first color in the center. Surround that with eight squares of the second color. Surround that with 16 squares of the first color. Sew each row together. Press seams flat.

3 Repeat step 2 for the other side of the pillow, beginning with a square of the second color in the center, surrounded by eight squares of the first color, surrounded by 16 squares of the second color.

4 Lay the two sides of the pillow together, with right sides facing each other. To eliminate any extra bulk, in each corner mark a dot ¾ inch (1.9 cm) in from each edge. Mark two more dots, 2¼ inches (5.7 cm) in from one edge and ¼ inch (0.6 cm) in from the other edge. Connect the three dots (figure 1). Repeat in each corner.

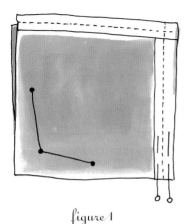

figure 1

5 Pin one side of the pillow together. Center your zipper on this seam, and mark the ends of the zipper with pins. Remove the zipper.

6 Beginning at one corner, backstitch a couple of stitches, and then stitch forward until you reach the pin marking one end of the zipper. Backstitch a couple of stitches. Lengthen your stitches as long as they'll go (basting stitches), and baste the seam together until you get to the pin marking the other end of the zipper. Stop. Shorten your stitches back to a sewing length, backstitch a couple of stitches, then stitch forward to the other corner. Backstitch and remove the pillow. Press the seam open.

7 Lay the closed zipper face down on the wrong side of the seam you just sewed, with the teeth running along the basted seam. Tape across the zipper at each end and a couple of times across the middle. Using the zipper foot, topstitch all the way around the zipper as close as the zipper foot allows you to get to the teeth. Remove from the machine, pull off the tape, and carefully pick open the basting stitches using a seam ripper.

8 Open the zipper and, with right sides together, pin the other three sides of the pillow together. Stitch the rest of the way around the pillow, and clip each corner. Turn the pillow right side out, and stuff in the insert. Then zip it up.

onetreehill

A few scraps of fabric and some embroidery floss combine to form this charming scene of blue sky, white cloud, green tree and hill, and scampering brown squirrel. Take this general technique and run with it to decorate your walls with your own peaceful vistas.

WHAT YOU NEED

Basic Patchwork Tool Kit (page 11)

Colored, patterned fabrics in aqua blue, lime green, and white

Thread in complementary colors

Embroidery floss in dark and light brown, dark and light green, light blue, dark and light coral

Embroidery needle

Embroidery hoop

8 x 8-inch (20.3 x 20.3 cm) wood canvas frame

Staple gun

SEAM ALLOWANCE

1/4 inch (0.6 cm)

DESIGNER

AIMEE RAY

WHAT YOU DO

1 Cut different sizes of squares and rectangles from the aqua fabrics. Piece them together at random to make a square at least 10 x 10 inches (25.4 x 25.4 cm).

2 Using the project photo as a guide, cut squares and rectangles from the green fabrics, and sew them together in rows, enough to cover the hill section of the picture. Fold over 1/4 inch (0.6 cm) of the edge of the green piece into a curve to make the hill shape and press. Use the appliqué stitch to sew the hill in place at the corner of the aqua square.

3 Cut a few more squares of green fabric, and sew them together. Cut the oval tree shape from this piece. Then cut two oval cloud shapes from the white fabric. Press the edges 1/4 inch (0.6 cm) in, and stitch them in place on the aqua background.

4 Embroider the tree trunk, hill and cloud lines, flowers, and squirrel as shown in the photo.

5 Center the art piece over the frame. Fold the sides over the back, and staple them in place with a staple in both the top and bottom and one in each side. Continue pulling the fabric tightly and stapling it down along each side of the frame.

ARTISTIC LICENSE

If you decide to design your own fabric masterpiece, remember that you're creating a 10-inch-square (25.4 cm) overall piece with an 8-inch (20.3 cm) square visible from the front.

templates

Tote - ally Cute

Page 75

Enlarge 200%

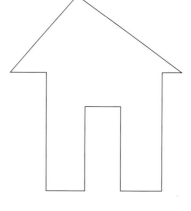

patchwork

flower

Home Sweet Home Coasters

Page 32

Enlarge 200%

Birdie Mobile

Page 102

Enlarge 300%

wing

large bird

small bird

Spiffy Potholders

Page 36

Enlarge 300%

strawberry

banana

leaf

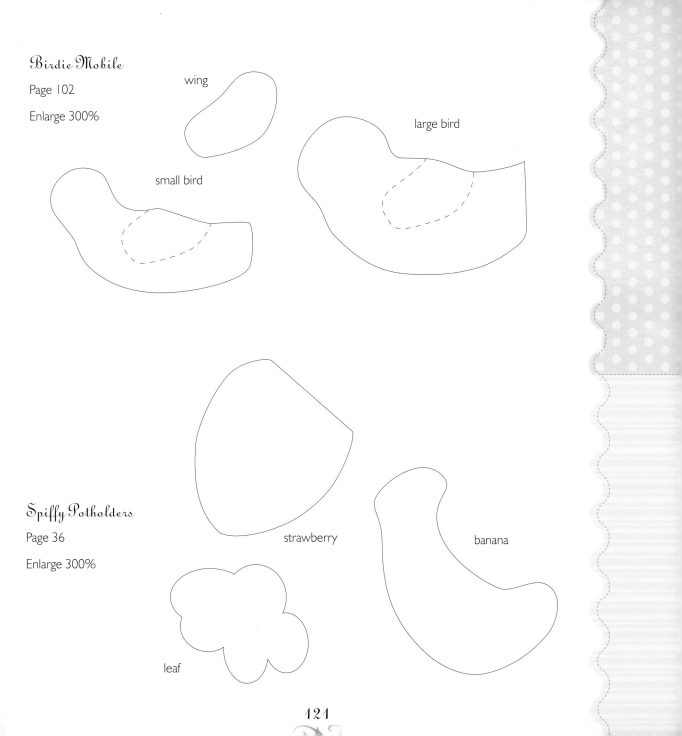

Perky Bird Coffee Jacket

Page 58

enlarge 200%

bird

 wing

sleeve

Hugs and Kisses Card

Page 34

Enlarge 300%

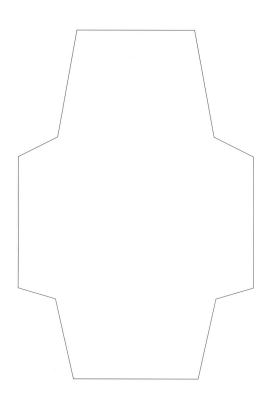

Starlet Pincushion

Page 29

actual size

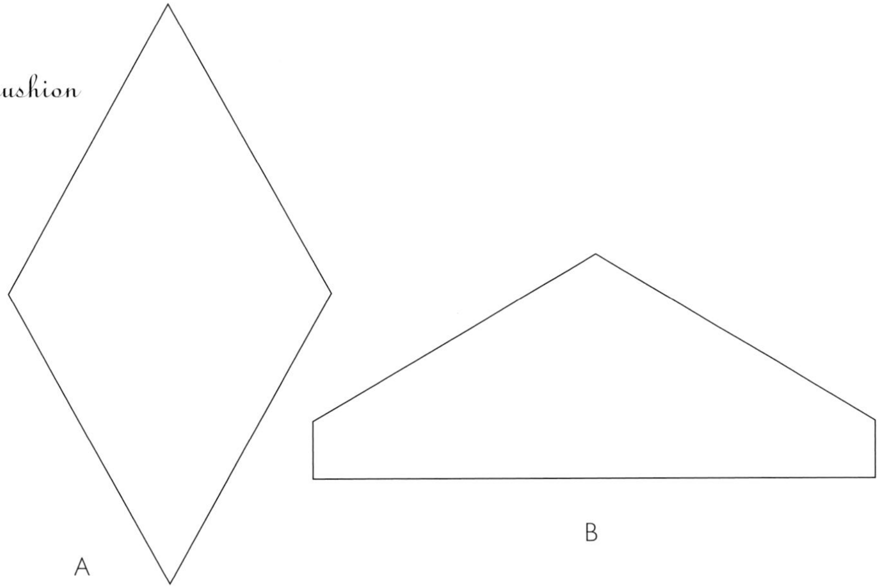

A

B

In the Bag

Page 63

Enlarge 200%

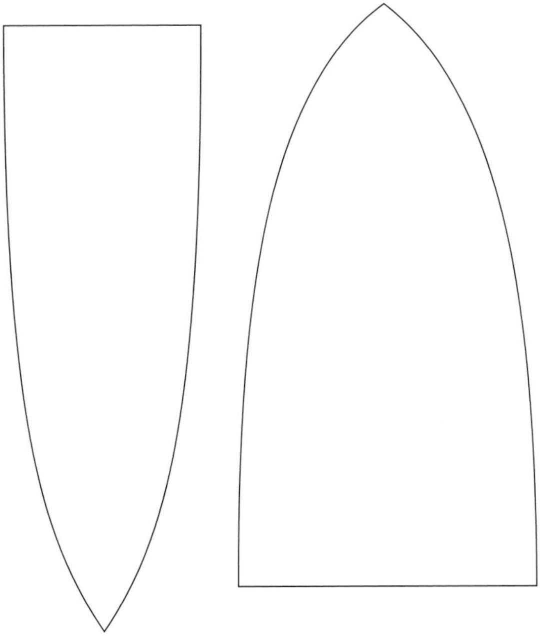

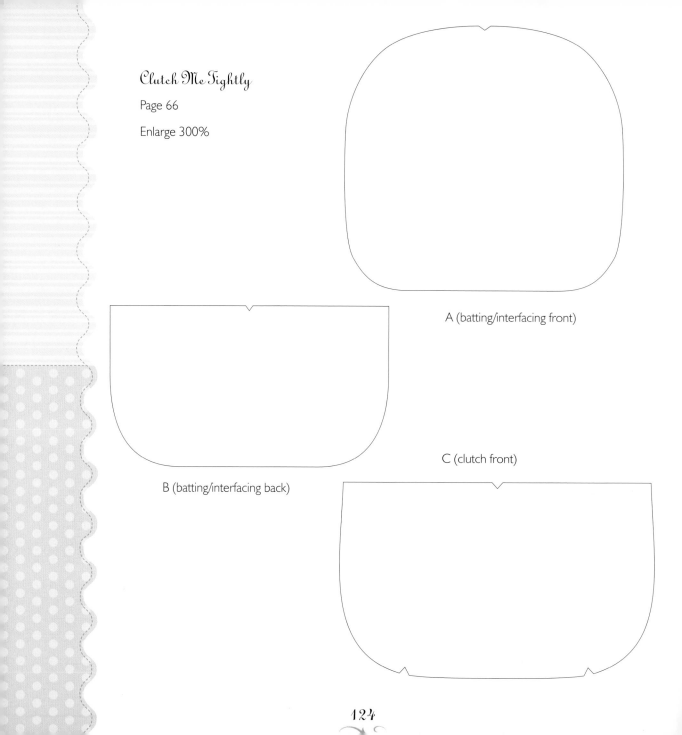

Clutch Me Tightly

Page 66

Enlarge 300%

A (batting/interfacing front)

B (batting/interfacing back)

C (clutch front)

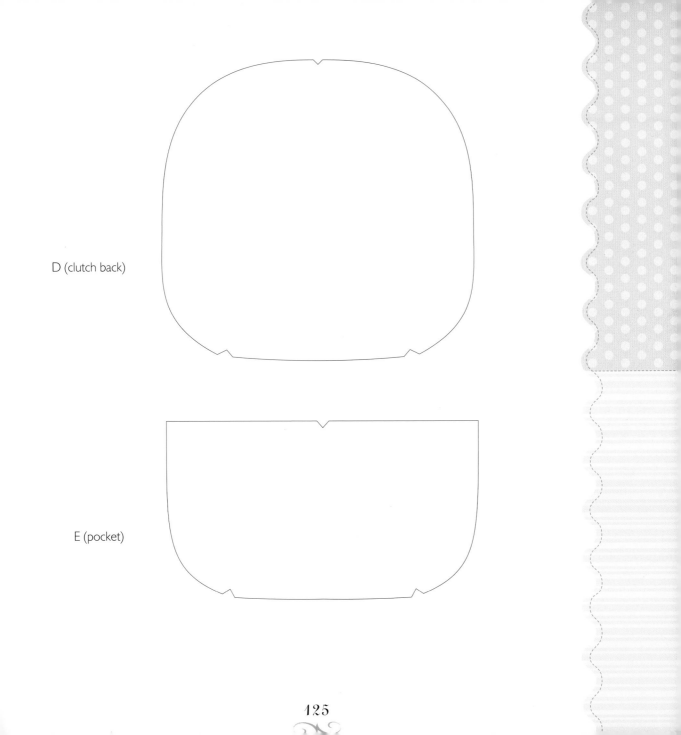

D (clutch back)

E (pocket)

about the designers

BELINDA ANDRESSON designs and handcrafts a range of contemporary patchwork cushions and accessories from her beachside home in Sydney, Australia. Her work is sold under the label Tuttifrutti at a number of retail stores in Australia, as well as online at www.modamuse.com.

WENDY ARACICH'S first major sewing projects included a milkshake-shaped pillow and a pair of boxer shorts in the fifth grade. Since then, she has covered the walls of a museum with a three-dimensional fiber sculpture, started a business selling crafts and cuteness, and amassed quite a stash of vintage buttons and rickrack. Wendy runs an online boutique, Circle Circle Dot Dot (www.circlecircledotdot.com).

MAITREYA DUNHAM is a scientist and teacher by day and a crafter by night. She posts her latest sewing, embroidery, crochet, or whatever other projects she's got cooking at craftlog.org. Maitreya is also a contributor to the collaborative craft blog Whip Up (whipup.net). Her work has appeared in the books The *Crafter's Companion* and *Pretty Little Potholders*. She lives in New Jersey with her husband, Mark, and two cats, Becket and el Chupacabra.

BRIDGET M. GOSS is pursuing her law degree from the University of North Carolina. As a little girl, Bridget would sit around the kitchen table with her mother and two sisters creating craft projects. She now enjoys releasing her creative energy by cooking for family and friends, planning weddings, and (still) creating craft projects.

WENDI GRATZ lives with her family and her sewing machine just down the road from the Penland School of Crafts in western North Carolina. Her first sewing project, a tablecloth, was a disastrous but educational experience. Her second project was designing and making all the costumes for a play. Now she makes fun clothes, funky dolls, and all kinds of quilts. You can see her work at www.wendigratz.com.

AUTUM HALL lives in North Carolina with her husband, two children, and too many pets to name. She took up sewing as a way to decorate on a budget in her own unique style. It wasn't long before her daughter started to put in requests for handbags. After her daughter's friends began asking as well, Autum began Daisy Goods, a small business designing unique handbags and home décor.

ERIN HARRIS, a stay-at-home mom to two young girls, lives in Louisville, Kentucky. She learned to sew in junior high school home ec and thinks it was the best class she ever took. Erin now sews, knits, crochets, and embroiders. You can follow her adventures in craft at www.houseonhillroad.com.

LAUREN HUNT was introduced to patchwork only recently, and she is trying to make up for lost time by obsessively purchasing more quilting cotton than she will ever be able to use. She exists on the Internet at www.auntjune.com, where you can read her blog or buy her handmade items. Lauren lives in Kansas City,

Missouri, with her extremely tolerant husband, Brian, and her disturbingly curious cat, Baxter.

REBEKA LAMBERT lives with her husband and three small children on the outskirts of Baton Rouge, Louisiana. She currently works in the IT field, though hopes to one day fulfill her dream of creating and designing full-time. You can catch a glimpse of her life on her blog, http://artsycraftybabe.typepad.com. She also has an online shop, www.artsycraftybabe.etsy.com, where she periodically sells her creations.

BETHANY MANN is a crafty mom who resides in the Santa Cruz Mountains in California with her husband, son, and a couple of cats. A former window dresser and file clerk, Bethany is currently obsessed with sewing clothes from vintage patterns, jewelry making and gardening. She spends lots of time haunting thrift stores and flea markets looking for raw crafting materials and a colorful anecdote or two for her blog at bitterbettyindustries.blogspot.com.

JOAN K. MORRIS'S artistic endeavors have led her down many successful creative paths, including ceramics and costume design for motion pic-

tures. Joan has contributed projects to numerous Lark books, including *Cutting Edge Decoupage* (2007), *Creative Stitching on Paper* (2006), *Exquisite Embellishments for Your Clothes* (2006), *Gifts For Baby* (2004), *Hardware Style* (2004), and *Hip Handbags* (2005).

RENEE PARRILL designs and sews in her studio in Columbus, Ohio, where she also helps her husband, Matt, run their tattoo business. Renee learned to sew in her family's upholstery shop, where she discovered that upholstery scraps make really sad Barbie clothes. Renee's focus now is on handbag design and construction, with an emphasis on themes from popular culture. When she's not sewing handbags, Renee likes to make things for her husband and their two daughters, Ailene and Emma. She can be contacted at www.flamestitch.com.

AIMEE RAY has been making things for as long as she can remember. She is a graphic designer in the greeting card and comic book industries, and her other interests range from digital painting and illustration to sewing stuffed animals, embroidery, and everything else in between. She is the author of *Doodle Stitching* (Lark, 2007), a book of contemporary embroidery designs and projects.

You can see more of Aimee's work at her website, www.dreamfollow.com.

DORIE BLAISDELL SCHWARZ has been wielding a needle and thread and designing in notebook margins since the second grade. A Jersey Shore native, Dorie now lives in a small town in Illinois called Farmer City with her husband and her daughter. She keeps a craft blog at tumblingblocks.net/blog/.

VALERIE SHRADER made a pair of pink culottes when she was 11 and has loved fabric ever since. Valerie is on the staff of Lark Books, and has written and edited many books related to textiles and needlework. She knits every now and then, too, and hopes that art quilts will be her next creative exploration.

RUTH SINGER is a British designer-maker who works with eco, recycled, and natural fabrics. She creates handmade fashion and interior textile accessories using traditional techniques inspired by historic textiles. In 2006, Ruth was selected by the Crafts Council as one of the best new makers of the year for Springboard at Origin, a showcase of emerging artists at the London Craft Fair. Find out more about her work at www.ruthsinger.com

TERRY TAYLOR is an editor and writer in Asheville, North Carolina. His creative work includes a wide variety of craft-projects-on-demand for more Lark Books than he could count. He has studied at John C. Campbell Folk School, Appalachian Center for Crafts, and Haystack Mountain School of Crafts.

SHANNON UDELL designs funky little fabric patches, dolls, art quilts, and other goodies from her home in California and sells them at her online store, Mukibubb Folklore Boutique, mukibubb.etsy.com. The blocky forms in her work derive from the items that Shannon remembers from her childhood home and garden, as well as from her now-grown daughters' artwork as young children.

acknowledgments

Thanks, first of all, to the talented designers who contributed their imaginative and beautiful patchwork projects to this book.

Thanks, also, to the book's editorial team: Valerie Shrader, Nathalie Mornu, Kathleen McCafferty, Jess Clarke, Jessica Boing, Shannon Roberts, and Larry Shea. The design and art production team of Megan Kirby, Travis Medford, and Jeff Hamilton provided a beautiful setting for the book's words and images.

A final thanks to those who added some lovely elements to the patchwork of these pages: illustrator Susan McBride, photographer Stewart O'Shields, and photography assistant and model Megan Cox.

index